LIVING OFF THE LAND

Country People 1850–1950

Frances Mountford

Merlin Unwin Books

First published in Great Britain by Merlin Unwin Books, 2013

Text and illustrations © Frances Mountford, 2013

Merlin Unwin Books Limited
Palmers' House, 7 Corve Street
Ludlow, Shropshire, SY8 1DB

www.merlinunwin.co.uk

A CIP record of this book is available from the British Library

Pages illustrated and designed by Frances Mountford
Printed and bound by Printworks International

ISBN 978-1-906122-58-4

CONTENTS

Small is the wren,
Black is the rook.
Great is the sinner
Who steals this book.

ACKNOWLEDGEMENTS

Thank you to my husband, Alan, for all his help and advice and to my sister, Christine Hills, for her interest and for urging me to complete the book. In memory of our dear lurcher dog, Rosie, who lay at my feet during much of the making of it.

Thanks to those who have provided information and assistance of various kinds: Frederick Burke, Joan Hopton, Eric Hughes, Crispin Harding-Rolls, David Neal, Sallie Small, Colin Markham, "Midge" Raybould, Betty Stoker, Phyllis White.

In appreciation of the many small museums that I have visited and enjoyed all round the country, including my local ones in Dorking and Horsham.

The last load at R. METCALF's Hall Bank Farm, at Oughterside, Aspatria, Cumberland. 1920's

JOHN HOAD, a carrier. From about 1875 to 1912 he travelled about 30 miles, twice a week, between Ockley (Surrey) and Southwark (London)

NOTE

Many of the illustrations are taken from old photographs and postcards bought at fairs and markets. Most of them bear no identification as to who the people in them might be

iv

INTRODUCTION

People have worked upon our countryside for hundreds of years deriving a living from its forests, hills, moors and marshes, and passing down well-honed skills and traditions as they did so. Methods continued for centuries, with only minor developments, experiments and changes.

Walking through the countryside before the end of the Second World War in 1945 one could hardly fail to see people engaged upon some task in the fields, often performed with the aid of horses. But huge changes were imminent. Tractors and large machines would soon replace the horses, the small machines and many of the men too. All manner of chemicals and other amazing aids to producing better crops and rearing more productive domestic animals were to be introduced within a very few years. As a consequence many of the old practical skills were no longer needed. They were now far too slow. The way of life that had continued for so long faded away.

Fortunately there was one invention that had been made in time to capture and to record the final hundred years of those people and their struggle on the land. The camera had come into popular use by the 1860's. This book was inspired by my collection of photographs taken in those days before everything changed. All classes of country folk were depicted and I have set them out here, right through the hierarchy, from squire to tramp. They were all a part of the landscape.

A Sail Reaper, 1901

Near Deal, Kent

One generation passeth away and another generation cometh but the earth abideth

Ecclesiastes

Oft did the harvest to their sickle yield,
Their furrow oft the stubborn glebe has broke;

How jocund did they drive their team afield!
How bow'd the woods beneath their sturdy stroke!

 Thomas Gray

The Squire and the Gentry

The **SQUIRE** was the major landowner of an area. Country life revolved round him and his family. He employed all manner of workers, many of them local people, from an array of indoor servants to those on the estate. He might employ an agent to run the estate in his absence. There were gamekeepers, stable-hands, foresters, gardeners and perhaps river bailiffs.

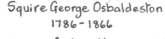

Squire George Osbaldeston 1786 - 1866

was a perfect gentleman and a renowned sportsman who owned vast Yorkshire estates. Although only 5 feet tall he was regarded as a superman, being a superb performer at all manner of sports: as race-rider, boxer, marksman, cricketer, huntsman, etc. He accomplished a 200 mile ride using 27 horses in 8 hours 42 minutes.

Some Squires were of the Peerage, holding estates passed down to them from early times. Other landlords had made their money from industry, such as coal mining or from iron works. These had bought land, built large mansions and set themselves up to live the same kind of lives as the Squires of long standing.

Sometimes a Squire happened to be the Parson too. In this case he was called the SQUARSON

The traditional SQUIRE lived largely off his estate. Rents came in from his tenanted farms. Produce for the house and keep for his horses came from the kitchen gardens and the Home Farm. His forests supplied wood for fences, tools and heating

THREE-QUARTERS OF THE COUNTRY WAS MANAGED IN THIS WAY

Writing in 1846 Alexander Somerville had high praise for the estates of Robert Peel (the Prime Minister), at Drayton Manor, Staffordshire. He saw good farming practices there and humanity shown to the working people. Similarly he had praise for Earl Spencer of Althorp Park, Nottinghamshire.

The Duke of Marlborough's estates were badly managed, while the Earl of Abingdon actually ejected poor people from his land.

Sir Robert Peel
1788 – 1850

John Charles
3rd Earl Spencer
1782 – 1845

Some of the great landlords set about making improvements in agricultural practices, by applying science to farming, and they occupied themselves in breeding superior livestock. Their results filtered down to the smaller farmers, particularly through Agricultural Societies and the Shows that they held

Between 1850 – 1880 country gentlemen lived comfortable lives. They had no high rates of income tax nor high estate duties.

THE GREAT DUCAL FAMILIES OWNED ABOUT 25% OF ALL ENGLAND

GENTRY OF A LOWER SOCIAL STATUS OWNED ANOTHER 30% AND YEOMEN AND SMALL PROPRIETORS WITH LESS THAN 1,000 ACRES EACH OWNED ABOUT 24%

The Rt. Hon. George Harry Grey, Earl of Stamford and Warrington, 1827–1883 owner of the Enville Hall estate in Staffordshire, enjoyed life as a fairly typical squire of his period. He was a fine athlete and horseman but excelled at cricket, being President of the Marylebone Cricket Club. He owned, at Enville, a ground which rivalled Lords. He also created 70 acres of ornamental gardens and built an enormous conservatory. The gardens attracted as many as 4,000 people a day when opened to the public in the 1850's and 60's.

The Honourable ladies VICTORIA and ALBERTINE GROSVENOR, daughters of the extremely wealthy Lord Ebury, photographed in a cart drawn by four donkeys at Moor Park, Rickmansworth, Herts. in about 1870.

GUY TEMPLE MONTACUTE NEVILL. (1883-1954), succeeded to the title of 4th Marquess of Abergavenny in 1938. Seen here in the hunting dress of the Eridge Hunt in Kent, of which, he became a Master of Hounds and in which county he lived.

LORD RIBBLESDALE, (1855-1925). His country estate was Gisburn Park, Lancs. He was a Liberal Whip in the House of Lords and Master of the Privy Buckhounds. Both of his sons were killed in the First World War.

"A squire himself and born of squires,
He bears, to Domesday-Book appealing,
A name well honoured in the Shires
For centuries of upright dealing;
His battlemented towers command
A stately pleasaunce, iron gated,
Where, at a former owner's hand
Good Queen Elizabeth was fêted."

THE COUNTRY SQUIRE. A. COCHRANE.

Many squires had very conservative ideas and kept up the old traditions.

They kept a close check on their estates, they attended the quarter sessions, the county ball and the races. They read newspapers and books on history, natural history and sporting subjects. They complained about the degeneration of the country, of old families being replaced in ancient houses by nobodys who had made money in trade and by the new railroads that spoiled their views.

In the 1880's the agricultural DEPRESSION affected the incomes of the gentry and they received a further blow in 1894 by the introduction of DEATH DUTIES. As a consequence some owners of large estates were obliged to sell off land and farms.

A lady and gentleman of the mid 1860's in a carefully posed photograph in front of a verandah. A table with a vase of flowers has been brought outside. She wears fashionable outdoor clothes, a posy of flowers rests on her lap and an umbrella against her knee. He sports a fringe beard but no moustache. His watchchain is especially thick and he was evidently a keen shot as he chose to be photographed carrying his gun.

4

"You must bark loudly if you see a gentleman coming"

from a lithograph of 1858

Enormous hooped crinoline skirts were severe handicaps to physical activity in the 1850's

Country Ladies

There was usually a busy social life, with house parties, field sports, tennis, croquet, archery, etc. Horses and dogs were important in their lives.

about 1905
A suit with the popular style Norfolk jacket.

about 1915
Woollen suit with fur wrap and pheasant feathers in the hat.

Leading her son on his pony, this lady has followed the North Cheshire Hunt on foot in about 1905.

GROOMS and COACHMEN

Grooms and Coachmen were essential to any large household before the use of the motor-car became general (from about 1900 for wealthy people).

The groom looked after the childrens' ponies, the hunters and hacks and the carriage horses. He donned coachman's livery to drive the family out in the carriage.

A groom with a good looking hunter, about 1910

about 1910

A handsome coachman, who no doubt, set many a housemaid's heart a-flutter.

A smart turn-out of the early 1900's

CARRIAGE Dog

Fashionable people liked to have Dalmatians trotting along by the carriage

When horse-drawn carriages were replaced with motor cars, grooms were still needed for the riding horses. Some grooms learned to drive a car and became "the engineer." "Perhaps he'll go with his nosebag on," people would mock when the car broke down. Later professional drivers were called "the chauffeur".

FIELD SPORTSMEN

Crops, poultry, specially reared game birds, desirable salmon and trout, and young animals such as lambs are constantly preyed upon by predators of one kind or another. Catching and killing these require much knowledge and skill. The pitting of wits, the outdoor endeavour and the social life that was generated in hunting the creatures was enjoyed by many, to such an extent that the quarry itself became conserved and provided with suitable habitat so that it could flourish in sufficient numbers to provide good hunting.

ONE OF THE MAJOR RECREATIONS OF COUNTRY PEOPLE LAY IN

SOME FORM OF HUNTING which encompassed:

SOCIAL CONTACT

KNOWLEDGE OF WILDLIFE AND COUNTRYSIDE

AN UNDERSTANDING OF HOUNDS AND HORSES

ADHERENCE TO TRADITIONS AND RULES

SKILL

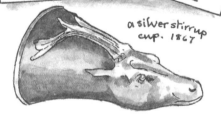
a silver stirrup cup. 1867

Will, somewhere near Aylesbury, Bucks. in 1907, with hare and a matched pair of greyhounds. (photo: J.T. Newman).

DEER • hunted in a few areas on horse-back with Staghounds or Buckhounds

OTTER • hunted on foot with Otterhounds

HARE • hunted on horseback with Harriers
• and on foot with Beagles or Bassets
• coursed with Greyhounds or Lurchers

FOX • hunted on horseback with Foxhounds
• and on foot in mountainous regions unsuitable for horses also with Foxhounds

FOX HUNTING

was the most popular
FIELD SPORT

— The GOLDEN AGE was from 1850 to 1915 —

With the fair wide heaven above outspread
  The fair wide plain to meet,
With the lark and his carol high over my head,
  And the bustling pack at my feet, —
I feel no fetter, I know no bounds,
  I am free as a bird in the air:
While the covert resounds, in a chorus of hounds,
  Right under the nose of the mare—

G.J. Whyte Melville

Many Squires were Masters of Hounds and with some of them fox hunting was an obsession. They lived for it, neglected their families, hunted several times a week and thought about horses and the breeding of hounds most of the time.

An elderly and feeble Squire has his favourite hounds brought into the house to see him.

Sketched from a painting by Gilbert S. Wright

Many could recite the bloodlines for generations back of every hound in the pack and could recognise the voice of each one. The "music" of the pack in full cry was made up of many voices: "I like a deep mouthed one that puts you in mind of looking into a bell, and makes the bass part of the sound, then the loud ringing mouth doubling an echo and coming in with its counter, and your soft mouth to fill in, eh?"   Thomas Miller. 1841

The famous Waterloo Run 2 February. 1866

ON A REALY GOOD RUN A FOX MIGHT GO FOR 25 MILES BEFORE BEING LOST OR CAUGHT
~ The Pytchley Hunt ~ Huntsman: Anstruther Thompson.

Hounds drew in Waterloo Gorse and they ran for 18 miles in 1 hour and 50 minutes without a check, then they ran for another 1 hour and 45 minutes. Anstruther Thompson rode 3 different horses, delivered to him by a groom, and he fell several times. He stopped hounds, without a kill, at 5.30pm, rode 19 miles back to kennels, ate his dinner, attended the Hunt Ball in Market Harborough and was hunting again next morning

THE FIELD

"There is nothing so good for the inside of a man as the outside of a horse."

Wheatland Hunt Button

The aptly named Rowland Hunt of Boreaston Park, Shropshire. His inherited estate had been bestowed for bravery on the battlefield of Shrewsbury in 1403. He was both Master and Huntsman of the Wheatland in the early 1890's. He liked to ride Arab Horses.

A Welsh Foxhound with a rough coat

Telephone: Montgomery, 9.

Mr. David Davies' Hunt.

Master: DAVID DAVIES, Esq. M.P.

Chairman of Committee:
W. SAVAGE, Esq.

Hon. Secretary:
Mr. CHAS. JAMES.

BRYNAWEL,
MONTGOMERY.

March 1930.

David Davies Hunt Button

The Master and the Hunt Servants wore red hunting coats (originally adopted from the uniforms of the Duke of Wellington's soldiers). A few Hunts wore other colours. They wore silk top hat or hunting cap, white breeches, white tie (stock) secured with a plain pin, which, for hunt staff was pinned vertically; a white, yellow or check waistcoat and black boots with brown tops.

Small details of dress were significant and absolute correctness of clothes was important according to one's position within the Hunt and to one's social class.

THE MASTER OF FOXHOUNDS (M.F.H.)

was sometimes a titled landowner or else a wealthy gentleman who bred the hounds and maintained them at his own expense. If not, the Hunt was run on a subscription basis and the Master was elected by a committee.

Foxhounds might sometimes be kept at local farms and collected up on hunting days but usually they were kept all together in Kennels

Almost the whole of England and Wales was divided into "countries", each covering several square miles. Some areas were not suitable, such as round the Wash and Industrial areas

The most fashionable packs were centred upon Melton Mowbray in Leicestershire, where the country had good grass fields and well-kept fences and plenty of coverts for foxes. The Quorn, Cottesmore, Belvoir and Pytchley were famous Hunts in that area.

Hunting Outfits c.1914

1935

Body and sleeves of coat lined with flannel, the skirt with cloth or waterproof material.

from a drawing by J.P. Thornton

Hunt Servants

a Victorian "swap"

Feeding the Hounds

The MASTER, or the HUNT COMMITTEE, employed a

HUNTSMAN

to hunt the pack. He was knowledgeable and skilled, understanding the ways of the fox and the control and directing of the hounds. His business, too, was to provide a good day out for the Field, with, if possible, a long and fast run.

Next in command after the HUNTSMAN was the WHIPPER IN, followed by the

SECOND WHIPPER IN, both of which were employed to assist the Huntsman. The Master, Huntsman and Whippers In wore the <u>hunt livery.</u>

The EARTH STOPPER blocked off holes that a fox might bolt into and unstopped them at the end of the day's hunting

The TERRIER MAN sent his terriers down a hole if a fox had gone to earth and it had to be killed.

A typical Huntsman of the early 20th century

Tommy Dobson, Eskdale Huntsman.

Dobson (1825-1910) founded the Ennerdale and Eskdale Hounds (a foot pack) in Cumbria himself, in 1883. He was a renowned Huntsman of his pack for 53 seasons.

In hilly regions, such as parts of Wales and the Lake District, horses could not be used. Huntsmen had to be fit and tireless to walk up and down steep slopes all day. A hill fox could kill many lambs

During the First World War most hunts kept going. At this time there were 12 female Masters and a few female Whippers In.

The Rest of the FIELD

The HUNTING FIELD brought social contact between all classes. Anyone could be a follower if he paid his subscription. Farmers whose land was hunted over did not normally pay a fee and foot followers paid nothing. A labourer might earn a penny or two when opening a gate for a lord.

The right to wear a red coat and the distinctive button of the particular Hunt, as worn by the hunt staff, was granted to only a few followers.

Farmers, and others, usually wore "ratcatcher", i.e. a tweed coat, brown breeches, brown or black boots, a top hat, or, later, a bowler. A shirt with a tie or neckcloth was acceptable.

1870 – from The Illustrated London News

After the 1914-18 WAR hunting was impeded to some extent because barbed wire became more common, making fences more dangerous to jump. More roads were tarmacked, which were hard on horses' hooves and carried faster traffic than before. Country estates began to break up because of financial problems. Nevertheless foxhunting was as popular as ever, with many Hunts managing to continue throughout the 1939-45 WAR

"Here's a health to "Sir George", who has found us the cover!
Here's a health to the farmers whose land we ride over!
Here's a health to "the customers", every one!
And to all the fair ladies who rode through the run!
Come close up, my sportsmen, a bumper toast fill!
Here's to Warwickshire Hounds, and old Shuckburgh Hill!"
1878 - Reg. Wyverne.

A fox-head stirrup cup.

The Ladies

a silver scent bottle of 1886

From the mid-1800's women were accepted on the Hunting Field.

They were greatly handicapped by having to ride side-saddle (for the sake of modesty) and in requiring a horse that was trained to take a side-saddle rider.

In 1860 a saddle with an extra pommel was introduced, which gave ladies a safer seat.

The RIDING HABIT was a dangerous hazard as well, as it was easily caught up on the saddle itself if the lady fell, and she could be dragged along the ground. In 1875 a skirt which detached at the waist was introduced, (which could provide an embarrassing sight if she were thrown). Other safety improvements followed.

In 1880 the Quorn Hunt made it compulsory for ladies to wear a new split safety skirt.

Habits were black or brown. Ladies did not usually wear red.

Photographed in Liverpool by E. Cox Walker in about 1870, this lady wears the usual top hat, with the veil here drawn up onto the hat brim. Her habit flows onto the floor as the hem was designed to be level when on horseback. It was made of heavy wool and lined with flannel. Underneath she would have worn a corset and a body stocking of silk or wool.

"Tally-ho!" A sketch by an unknown artist.

"Long limber and grey, see him stealing away,
Half a minute and then 'Tally-ho!'"

A great many women rode well and hunted, enjoying the thrill and danger of a fast run over fences. Some avoided being in at the kill The first WOMAN M.F.H. was Lady Salisbury in the early 1870's. The second was Victoria, Countess of Yarborough, from 1875-80.

It was not until the 1920's that riding astride became acceptable for women. By the 1930's 60% of the Field was female.

WHEN THE WIND IS WEST, THE FISH BITE BEST

ANGLERS

IN ENGLAND AND WALES THERE ARE ABOUT 38 SPECIES OF FRESHWATER FISH IN RIVERS AND PONDS

Enjoy thy stream,
    O harmless fish,
And when an angler for his dish
Through gluttony's vile sin,
Attempts, a wretch, to pull
        thee out
God give thee strength,
    O gentle trout,
To pull the raskall in!
            J. Wolcott

alder fly

GAME FISHING: for TROUT and SALMON in rivers and lakes — usually for the wealthy.

COARSE FISHING: for CARP, BREAM, TENCH, etc. in still water — especially popular with town people.

— TROUT —
The season, the weather, changing light, the insects on which the fish feed, must all be studied, and skill to cast the fly acquired.

— SALMON —
Many varieties of flies and techniques can be used to tempt the fish. When hooked they might break the line and escape — a great challenge

FISHING FOR TROUT c.1900
Before 1920 rods were long, to reach well out across the river, and made from a variety of woods and whalebone, later from split bamboo. Lines easily tangled. Oiled silk lines replaced the earlier horsehair. In 1920 an efficient reel was introduced which prevented the line from tangling.

"The cool water meadows, the setting sun, with its golden glow on the water, add a peculiar charm to fishing at this time of day in the hot summer months. And then — the splash of your fish as you hook him! How magnified is the sound in the dim twilight, when you cannot see, but can only hear and feel
        your quarry."   J.A. Gibbs. 1912

In 1922 Georgina Ballantine, a small woman, had a 2 hour struggle to land a 64 lb salmon, (the largest ever caught), from a boat, in the Tay in Scotland.

A proud angler with a salmon, 1920's

13

SHOOTING MEN

the [1860's] Shooting Clothes in were of plain or checked tweed, long loose jackets and full breeches worn with leather boots, leggings, or knee socks and stout shoes

About [1912] from a drawing by J.P. Thornton, a Master Tailor

The "Norfolk" jacket was popular for many years for sporting folk and other country people because the pleats, both front and back, gave good ease of movement

Before 1860 a landowner liked to walk over his estate with his gun and his dog, and perhaps with a few friends too, to shoot any game that might be found, according to the season.

There were usually birds in abundance, as farming practices on the small, hedged, fields, that were worked mostly by manual labour and with natural fertilisers, favoured the breeding of all birds and wildlife.

Woodcock and Snipe were challenging shots even for very experienced sportsmen.

The term "GAME" covered a great many varieties of birds on heath, moor, field and in covert, as well as the "GROUND GAME" of hares and rabbits.

~ FORMS of SHOOTING ~

1. With a dog working in front of the gun which either points at or flushes out the game. (Rough Shooting)

2. Several men walking in a line and shooting the game as it flies up of its own accord ("Walking up")

3. Lines of "beaters," usually local men recruited for the day, who drive the birds towards the waiting, stationary guns. ("Driven" shooting)

4. WILDFOWLING. Shooting on marsh, shore, mudflats, estuaries, etc, for waterbirds such as geese, duck, widgeon, etc.
The Shoreshooter waited for birds to fly in, often he used decoys.
The Puntgunner stalked birds in the marshes by lying concealed in a punt.

5. Other shooting encompassed shooting rabbits, often aided by a ferret or a dog; shooting pigeons, perhaps from a hide and using decoys; shooting vermin and the predators of conserved and specially reared game.

Organised shooting, such as Driven Game Shooting, began in about 1860 (probably in East Anglia), but many true sportsmen preferred the old ways and did not care for the birds to be driven towards the guns by a line of beaters.

"I am an old fogey and cannot take up very easily with new fashioned ideas, and I would. I candidly admit, sooner not shoot at all as shoot without dogs, or with only a retriever held in slip. And as to walking along in a line with a dozen other men, why, I would rather go into the Volunteers and do so many hours drill......
I prefer to shoot alone, or with one or two old fashioned fellows like myself, and over dogs........
Dead slow no doubt; but I get my walk, I see the beautiful instinct of the dogs, and what faculties education can develop in them, and I get as many birds as I want."

"N" in Baily's Monthly Magazine, October 1879.

Rough Shooting for grouse with a pointer, 1877 (A watercolour by an unknown artist/sportsman).

Young sportsmen with assorted dogs and puppies, about 1920 (from a snapshot)

Before 1880 a sporting landlord could rear as much game as he liked and allow it to roam over the land, eating his tenants' crops. It was illegal for farmers to kill the hares, rabbits, etc.

The GROUND GAME ACT 1880 gave occupiers of land the right to take hares

RABBITS were bred in warrens in medieval times and later

kept in estate parks for their decorative qualities, as well as for food. In time they over-ran the countryside, denuding the crops and the woodlands, as well as undermining the ground with burrows and eating food that reared-game fed on. Gamekeepers killed vermin that attacked the game, so rabbits benefited from this and increased even more, becoming a serious pest on farmland.

Landlords and their tenant farmers were often at logger-heads over the damage done to crops. Many farmers negotiated the right to destroy those on the land they rented.

As they were so plentiful, numbers were difficult to reduce. Most country folk felt no guilt about poaching a few for the pot. If they were caught the penalties for taking rabbits were not as high as for catching other types of game. There was no closed season for killing rabbits.

from a faded photograph

An estate employee or a farm worker, who, no doubt had permission to shoot over local land, returns home with a few rabbits for pies and stews.

GAMEKEEPERS

The Gamekeeper was the elite of the Estate employees.

Immaculately turned out in about 1896

from a faded cabinet card photo.

His WORK:

to rear and to protect game of all kinds so that it could eventually be shot by the landlord and his friends, as well as to provide game for use in the kitchens.

○

He learned his work by starting as a keeper's Lad. He prepared food for the birds, scrubbed out hutches, fed and watered the hens used for hatching and he learned to keep his eyes open for predators of all kinds.

○

On large estates several keepers were employed, one being the Head Keeper.

○

Catching predators, i.e. vermin, birds and human POACHERS, was a major concern for a keeper.

Early in the year the keepers collected eggs from the pheasant hens that had been penned, and they placed the eggs to be hatched under broody domestic hens that had been bought from local farms and cottages. The keeper and his assistants spent many hours feeding the newly hatched poults with special rations, protecting them, supervising the coops. Later they fed them in the rearing fields and then in the woods.

Partridges were sometimes reared, but this was very time consuming. Eggs from natural nests were collected and replaced with dummies. The eggs were hatched under bantams, where they could be protected. The chicks were replaced in the wild nests.

17

The GAMEKEEPER, in the latter part of the 1800's and in the 1900's, aimed to provide plenty of birds and good sport for the shooting parties held by his employer. The birds for these were usually pheasants or partridges. In moorland areas grouse were conserved. Their breeding and numbers were encouraged by the burning of heather to produce young heather shoots, that, with berries is their principal food. The keepers eliminated predatory raptors, such as eagles and hawks.

In the early 1900's gamekeeping reached its peak with an enormous number of birds being reared in some counties, and a great many keepers being employed.

Grouse-feather.
(dark brown with tan markings)

THE SHOOT. The Head keeper was in charge at the Shooting Party. Gangs of local people, recruited as Beaters drove the birds towards the waiting guns. Many of the guests invited to shoot were not countrymen, but wealthy industrialists, businessmen, politicians, etc. On these occasions the Keepers met many influential and famous people. Norman Mursell, on the Duke of Westminster's estate, was proud to have stuck a pheasant's feather in Winston Churchill's hat.

In late Victorian and Edwardian times, when shoots were large and fashionable, they amounted to a veritable slaughter of birds, rather than the reaping of a useful harvest.

Usually only land-owners, farmers and gamekeepers carried guns in the country

The Gamekeeper and the Huntsman both worked for the same land-owner. Both provided sport. Although the fox took birds and eggs the keeper had to try to let the fox live for hunting

by Mark Beaufoy.
Stops and beaters
oft unseen
Lurk behind some
leafy screen,
Calm and steady
always be,
NEVER SHOOT WHERE
YOU CAN'T SEE.

KEEPERS were disliked by local workers, who, while hoping to be taken on as beaters at shooting time, liked to catch a cheap dinner in the woods. In his job as protector of the game, a keeper would kill any cat or dog straying onto the estate

He was distrusted. People were hostile.

A Keeper's GIBBET on which he hung dead weasels, hawks, rats, crows, etc., all predators of his birds

A threatening-looking keeper, about 1920

18

MR. HUGH HUGHES ~ a keeper

1868-1930

Hugh Hughes worked first for 'old aristocracy', the Vaughans of Plas Gwyn, Pentraeth. In about 1908 he went, as gamekeeper, to Mr "Eynie" Palethorpe at the Palethorpe's Shooting Lodge in West Anglesey, which had 24 square miles of land. Mr Palethorpe was 'nouveau riche', having made his money as a butcher specialising in sausages.

Hugh Hughes job entailed maintaining the buildings of the Lodge and kennels. He repaired footbridges, stiles and hides. He hired casual labour to carry out the work, and beaters for the shoots, etc.

He had his cottage rent free and was supplied with free coal; he had a suit of clothes, boots, long stockings, hat and all the necessary accoutrements of a gamekeeper; a good gun and telescope. He was able to afford a pony and trap.

His cottage had its own few acres where he kept a cow, chickens and ducks. The out-houses contained dogs that he trained, not only for the Palethorpes but for other gentlemen who were members of the shoot. These dogs were sent in crates by train from the English Midlands to Ty Croes station and he was well paid for his services. He trapped rabbits and reared pheasants, the latter on land adjoining the Shooting Lodge, which was a large house overlooking the 'bog' of the River Crigyll. Eric Hughes, grandson.

The SHOOTING LAND that he looked after centred upon the River Crigyll, which had a bog at the seaward end, opening out onto Towyn Trewan Common. This provided all types of wildfowl. The rest of the land included large areas of gorse which were used for the driven shooting of pheasants.

Working for the Palethorpes, Hugh Hughes and other staff received boxes of sausages, hams and pies at Christmas, that arrived for them by train.

At a shoot dead and injured birds were retrieved by human "pickers up" and by dogs.

19

POACHERS

KEEP OUT
TRESPASSERS
WILL BE
PROSECUTED

On a night that is dry, when the wind's in the west,
And the moon will have set in an hour;
Oh, he says to his mates, "While the world is at rest
We'll away, and the countryside scour.
We've nets for the rabbit, the partridge, the hare,
The heathcock and pheasant as well,
Though keepers may watch them,
The poacher will catch them.
By river, vale, moorland and fell."
        J. M. Denwood

1828 Night Poaching Act – no unlawful killing of game by night
1831 Game Act – no killing of game on Sundays or Christmas Day

POACHERS usually operated at night, silently and secretly to steal game.
They hunted with dogs, guns, nets, all kinds of traps and snares, catapults and throwing-sticks, that were sometimes weighted at one end.

late 1860's
from photo by Norris, Birmingham.

A WALKING STICK/GUN
with which a poacher hoped to fool anyone that he was simply out for an innocent walk.

about 4' 6" long

brown wooden stock

There were also folding guns that could be hidden under a coat

metal barrel

POACHERS were often poor local men intent upon catching a dinner for a hungry family waiting at home. Men from towns nearby, perhaps out of work, went poaching for game to sell, while others were gypsies who lived from anything they could pick up.

THE KEEPER AND THE POACHER WERE ALWAYS AT WAR, WITH THE TRESPASSER SOMETIMES PUTTING UP A DESPERATE FIGHT RATHER THAN GIVING IN AND SPENDING A SPELL IN PRISON. KEEPERS' LIVES WERE IN DANGER AND INJURIES DID OCCUR

A poacher would conceal his gun, nets and the game he had caught in a ditch, a hollow tree or under brambles if he sensed danger. His dog would slink away. A small feather on the ground or a patch of bent grass might make a keeper suspicious and give the game away.
IT WAS ALWAYS A BATTLE OF WITS AND OF SKILLS BETWEEN POACHER AND KEEPER.

Bygones Museum,
Holkham Hall, Norfolk.

The poacher regarded pheasants, hares, etc. as belonging to no one, even though they were reared or protected by the landowner and his gamekeepers.

In an unfamiliar wood the wind and the stars were the poacher's guide and his dog a willing assistant.

Those that hunted hare ran them down with a pair of greyhounds or they used a lurcher to drive them towards a net stretched across a gateway.

A dog and a wonder is Sweep, I'll be bound;
  His marrow is not on the earth to be found,
How he arches his back and erects his great tail
When the scent of a hare is borne down on the gale;
At a wave of the hand he will speed through the night,
And make the bold poacher's heart throb with delight.

Hurrah! though the rich to the land may lay claim,
The world's a preserve ever filled with fat game,
And where is the dog that has slain such a heap
In double the lifetime of gallant old Sweep?

                    J. M. Denwood

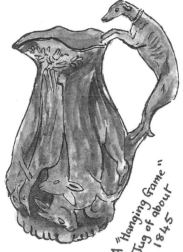

A "Hanging Game" Jug of about 1845

FARMERS

Then, boyhood past, he settled down
  with Annie for his wife—
And now he had his cares and toils,
  and anxious was his life;
For sometimes drought would vex his
  heart, or floods of rain would fall,
Sometimes he had a heavy crop, and
  sometimes none at all.

D.B.McKeen, 1884

A Victorian Scrap

The GENTRY owned most of the land.
The FARMERS usually rented it and generally worked on it in person.

● **WEALTHY FARMERS** with large acreages socialised with the gentry to a small extent but their lack of education and rough manners usually held them apart. Those with a great many acres often employed a bailiff to run the farm, which gave them time for other business, perhaps in local politics or in field sports. Like some members of the gentry, they were often interested in improvements in stockbreeding and developments in agriculture.

● **SMALL FARMERS** with about 100 acres or less worked on the land themselves with the help of their families or one or two labourers. They were often mixed farmers, keeping a pig or two, a small number of cattle, some poultry in the farmyard and they sowed some of their fields with arable crops. If their land was suitable they might specialise in sheep or dairy cows.

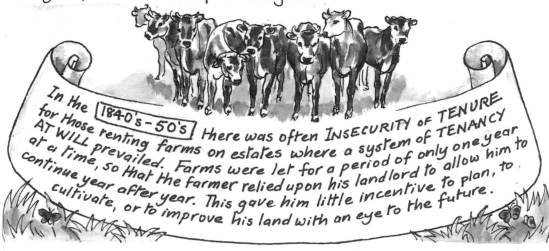

In the 1840's - 50's there was often INSECURITY OF TENURE for those renting farms on estates where a system of TENANCY AT WILL prevailed. Farms were let for a period of only one year at a time, so that the farmer relied upon his landlord to allow him to continue year after year. This gave him little incentive to plan, to cultivate, or to improve his land with an eye to the future.

22

Repeal of the CORN LAWS giving FREE TRADE — 1846

The country had kept pace in growing enough corn to feed the population, but the population was rapidly expanding and there was starvation in Ireland when the potato blight took hold. There had been many Corn Laws which regulated inland trade, exportation and the prohibition of importation. Now they were repealed, with the idea that, with extra corn being imported, bread would be cheaper for the hungry people. Some farmers feared that corn brought into the country would decrease the value of their home-grown crops. Others saw that British goods could be sold in exchange for imports. The FULL EFFECT of the REPEAL was not felt until the 1870's

Alexander Somerville, travelling in Dorset, Wiltshire and Somerset in 1846 found the farmers there hospitable, joyous and "uproariously free hearted" but generally they possessed only a "feeble glimmering of knowledge on commercial subjects"

On a stage-coach journey in the West Country he encountered a good-natured farmer from Somersetshire, whose large farm was assessed at £70 for the purpose of paying the Poor Rate. Somerville asked if he were a grazier or a corn grower. "I am both, more the pity," he replied, "because between falls in the prices of corn and falls in the prices of cattle, buying dear and selling cheap, I don't know what to be at with myself."

By 1850 the Stage-Coaches were almost at an end as the Railroads expanded all over the country. Roads that had formerly been busy grew over with weeds and inns closed.

The "Golden Age of Agriculture", 1853-62 came about as a result of farmers benefiting from various new developments such as improved roads and the increasingly expanding railway network, as well as scientific discoveries which affected agriculture. Steam power could be applied to drive machines and it was now realised that certain kinds of soil suited some crops more than others.

When the first English Agricultural Show, the Bath and West of England, was held in 1777 the animals had been judged on their pleasing appearance but then came breeding programmes to improve both stock and plants by such people as Robert Bakewell of Leicestershire and Thomas Coke at Holkham Hall in Norfolk. Agricultural Societies increased in number, bringing farmers together at their Shows, Gatherings and Dinners, so helping to spread Knowledge.

FARMERS remained PROSPEROUS throughout the 1860's, with the wealthiest of them improving their stock, particularly in breeding better sheep and cattle.

In 1865 there was a serious cattle plague that killed animals all over the country

At about this time a clinical thermometer was first used on animals and it was discovered that a rise in temperature was associated with disease

A farmer of Surrey who is proud to wear his smock frock and has a fine beaver hat on the table. Well polished boots and a good stick proclaim him as a respectable man of good standing from a photograph.

A Field Requires Three Things:
Fair Weather, Sound Seed and
A Good Husbandman

MOVING IN, MOVING OUT

Farms, both rented and owned, often passed down in families from generation to generation. Every county had its own customs as to the time of year that an old tenant could move out and a new tenant move in. There was also the question as to whether or not the incomer could gain access or "pre-entry" to prepare for the cultivation of certain crops, or if the outgoer could "hold over" to gain benefit from crops he himself had planted. He might be able to pick the apple crop or thresh his corn in the barn after officially quitting.

The usual dates for the change over of tenants were:

CANDLEMAS DAY · 2 February · eg. *Cumberland, Lancashire, Herefordshire, Monmouthshire.*

LADY DAY · 25 March · *a popular time in many counties*

OLD LADY DAY · 6 April · eg. *Lincolnshire*

MICHAELMAS DAY · 29 September · *popular in many counties*

OLD MICHAELMAS DAY · 11 October · eg. *Dorsetshire, Cambridgeshire, parts of Kent*

CHRISTMAS DAY · 25 December · eg. *some in Monmouthshire and Herefordshire*

Two of the wealthier class of country men mounted on good-looking hunters.
They do not wear special riding clothes.
late 1860's

1870~75 SAW A PEAK IN THE PROSPERITY FOR FARMING, BUT IN **1875** A **DEPRESSION** BEGAN WHICH LASTED FOR

20 YEARS

particularly affecting those in corn growing areas.

FREE TRADE made itself felt as the more efficient sea and railway services made the transportation of wheat from the prairies of America, Australia and Russia much cheaper. As a result, British farmers could not make a profit on it.

Some survived by laying their land down to grass and increasing their milking herds.

LABOURERS were pitifully poor as farmers could only afford to pay them very low wages.

A "John Bull" type of man, bewhiskered and portly.
Drawn from a faded carte-de-visite photograph
taken in the 1870's by Fred Wellsted of
Retford, Nottinghamshire

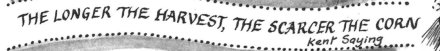

THE LONGER THE HARVEST, THE SCARCER THE CORN
Kent Saying

There was a succession of wet years with bad harvests. Cattle caught pleuro-pneumonia and Foot and Mouth disease, whilst sheep suffered from "liver rot." 1879 was a particularly bad year — cold and wet from beginning to end.

Many old traditions were dying out in the 1870's. Harvest festivals became more simple celebrations than formerly. Plough Monday was not always observed and other customs reduced in importance.

At the beginning of the 1870's Rents were high but farmers were doing well. However

as the DEPRESSION took hold large numbers of tenants on corn-growing land found they could not pay their rents, so both landlords and farmers faced ruin. With tenants in such straitened circumstances the landlords were obliged to reduce rents in order to keep tenants on the farms and, in consequence, tended.

Those on mixed farms fared better as there was no foreign competition in milk. Meat, which needed refrigeration, was not easily imported so fields that had previously grown wheat were laid down to grass for raising cattle. Money could still be made by growing fruit, and crops such as potatoes, cabbages, oats and barley, etc.

An unknown man of the early 1870's. He wears a good quality thigh-length coat and a long waist-coat with a high neck, dating back in style to ten or more years earlier. He has buttoned knee-breeches and leggings. From his expression one might judge that he was acute in business and drove a hard bargain.

100 acres of arable, ploughed and planted, could feed 150 PEOPLE for a year

100 acres of grassland, supporting cattle or sheep, could feed 15 PEOPLE for a year

"Nowhere are the classes so distinctly defined as in the country," wrote Richard Jefferies in the 1870's. Farmer and Squire rarely visited one another and the labourer no longer ate with the farmer and the family where he was employed.

UNPROFITABLE TIMES ~ For about ten years: 1880-1890

prices were still falling due to the increase in imports which made farmers' profits low. Continual bad weather and disease of livestock did not help matters, but farmers in some areas did not fare as badly as others.

FROM LABOUR HEALTH FROM HEALTH CONTENTMENT SPRINGS. A badge of 1884

A MAN SHOULD LIVE WITHIN HIS HARVEST

Success to the farmer,
The plough and the flail;
May the landlord flourish
And the tenant never fail

A farm wedding of about 1885 with ladies in fashionable tight-sleeved dresses and tall hats.

Country clothes of the mid 1800's: low crowned bowler hat; high buttoned waistcoat, cut-away jacket and a neckerchief

from a carte de visite

The grey mare pricks her well-pleased ear;
As rise our voices strong and clear;
The farm-house waits with table spread;
Cheer, brothers, cheer, our task is sped!
Home! Harvest Home! The "Open Hand"
Has scattered plenty through the land:
All praise to Him whose bounty given
Is pledge to us of Rest in Heaven.

Ashley H. Baldwin, 1884

Corn Idol of Wheat and Oats

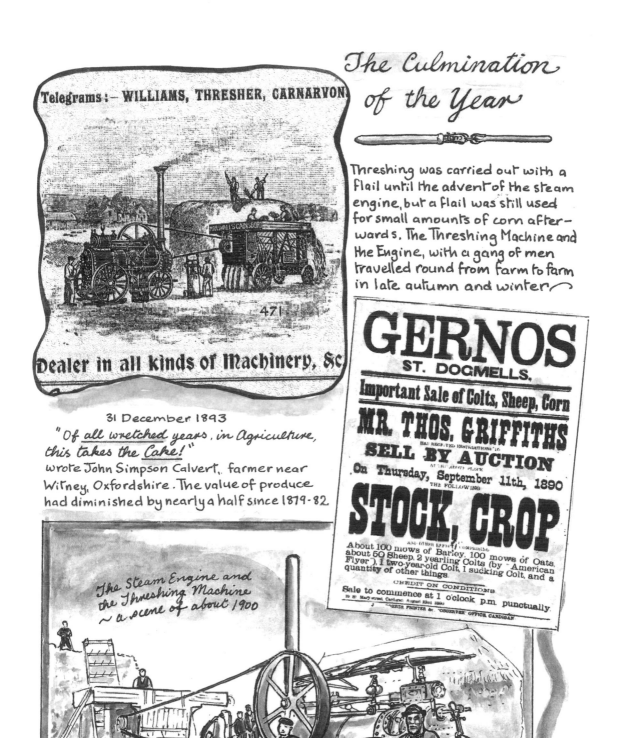

Telegrams:– WILLIAMS, THRESHER, CARNARVON.

471

Dealer in all kinds of Machinery, &c.

Threshing was carried out with a flail until the advent of the steam engine, but a flail was still used for small amounts of corn afterwards. The Threshing Machine and the Engine, with a gang of men travelled round from farm to farm in late autumn and winter.

31 December 1893

"Of _all wretched_ years, in Agriculture, this takes the _Cake!_" wrote John Simpson Calvert, farmer near Witney, Oxfordshire. The value of produce had diminished by nearly a half since 1879-82.

GERNOS
ST. DOGMELLS,
Important Sale of Colts, Sheep, Corn
MR. THOS. GRIFFITHS
HAS RECEIVED INSTRUCTIONS TO
SELL BY AUCTION
AT THE ABOVE PLACE
On Thursday, September 11th, 1890
THE FOLLOWING
STOCK, CROP
AND OTHER EFFECTS COMPRISING
About 100 mows of Barley, 100 mows of Oats, about 50 Sheep, 2 yearling Colts (by "American Flyer"), 1 two-year-old Colt, 1 sucking Colt, and a quantity of other things.
CREDIT ON CONDITIONS
Sale to commence at 1 o'clock p.m. punctually.

The Steam Engine and the Threshing Machine ~ a scene of about 1900

1914 ~ 1918 the First World War

Farming had made a steady recovery into the early 1900's, with livestock replacing corn in many areas.

A photograph of three who may have been a sister and her brothers. about 1918

YOUR COUNTRY'S NEEDS REQUIRE YOU

ONE & ALL

TO SOW EVERY AVAILABLE PIECE OF LAND WITH RELIABLE SEEDS.

With the coming of WAR British ships were sunk by the Germans and tons of imported food went to the bottom of the sea. By December 1916 the State intervened to increase the production of food at home. WAR AGRICULTURAL COMMITTEES, with DISTRICT COMMITTEES were set up to persuade and assist farmers to plough and cultivate their grassland in order to produce corn and potatoes. These would feed more people than livestock could per acre.

Many men and horses had gone to the war, leaving farmers very short of labour

A Soldier on leave helps out with the harvest.

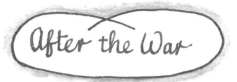

After the War

Farmers were doing well. The government had encouraged agriculture during the war and it continued to guarantee a minimum price for grain afterwards.

Many who could raise the capital bought their own farms. Prices of land and stock were high, but farmers were optimistic for future prosperity.

After 1921 the government cancelled the minimum guaranteed price, but labourers' wages were fixed at a minimum rate. Soon farmers were in financial difficulties, especially those who had bought their farms.

Farmers did not anticipate the slump which began in 1922 Prices of land and stock fell dramatically, and, ten years later were generally worth one quarter of their former values.

1926-27 "We employed one full-time man, plus many casual workers, both male and female — and their offspring! In the 1926-7 miners' strike we had 8 or 10 miners walking or cycling from Cannock Chase at least 10 miles away. Some slept rough in the farm buildings. All this for 4 shillings a day for harvesting the potato crop. Either that or starve!

Frederic Burke, farmer, near Aldridge. Staffordshire.

The Miners' Strike, for higher wages, culminated in the General Strike which seriously affected the whole country. While on strike the workers had no money.

LEGGINGS

Shaped to the leg, with winding strap. Leather. early 1900's

(or GAITERS) made of canvas, thick cloth leather, etc. were made in many styles.

"HE IS READY TO THE LAST GAITER BUTTON" i.e. well prepared

They were worn by country men of all classes, from labourers working in the fields to the gentry for country sports, to protect the lower leg from mud and thorns.

photographed in MACCLESFIELD

Over-the knee, in canvas or suede.

Tubular, thick canvas or leather

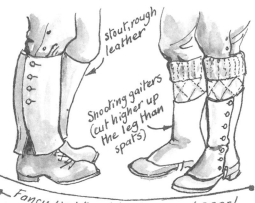

stout, rough leather

Shooting gaiters (cut higher up the leg than spats)

← Fancy waistcoat buttons and pearl legging buttons in Macclesfield. c.1880

PUTTEES
(from Hindi: patti = bandage)
From early times workers on the land wrapped cloths round their legs for rough work.
PUTTEES were long strips of cloth wound round the lower leg by infantry men and mounted soldiers, and occasionally adopted by farmers and farm workers, especially after the First World War.

By 1925 RUBBER BOOTS became popular in the USA, but in Britain "gumboots" or rubber "Wellingtons" did not replace leather boots-with-leggings as they were uncomfortable for all-day wear. After 1945 leggings were worn less as farm work became more and more mechanised.

~ Farmers' Diaries on the Isle of Wight ~

In the Arreton Valley, the most fertile part of the Isle of Wight, four generations of the BLAKE family kept diaries of the work they carried out on BIRCHMORE and STONE FARMS

JAMES RUFFIN BLAKE (1833-1900), of the third generation, was not only a highly efficient farmer who would work in the fields with his men, but also an educated gentleman who held several public offices.

A wide variety of crops was grown on the two farms and he kept Dorset Horn sheep which thrived on the chalk downland above the arable acres.

1858 Steam Threshing
1861 Ploughing Match at Stone Farm
1868 Cattle Plague
1879 The worst Harvest since 1816

December 1860 Honeymoon in London

He took his bride twice to Baker Street Cattle Show

and once to the Metropolitan Cattle Market They also visited Madame Tussauds and the Great Exhibition

Arreton Church.

JAMES RUFFIN SCOTT BLAKE (1872-1905) succeeded his father. He died after a long period of bad health, but for a few years he managed the farms and kept the diary going for most of the time.

The figures 6. 2. etc. denote the number of horses used. L or S etc. indicates the particular man in charge of the job.

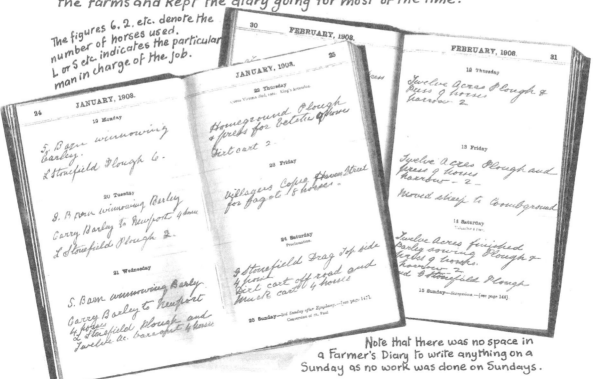

Note that there was no space in a Farmer's Diary to write anything on a Sunday as no work was done on Sundays.

The **NATIONAL FARMERS' UNION** held its first meeting on 10th December 1908, after a small group of farmers had banded together to form the Lincolnshire Farmers' Union in 1904 in an effort to overcome the general decline in agriculture

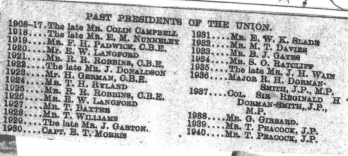

PAST PRESIDENTS OF THE UNION.

1908–17..The late Mr. COLIN CAMPBELL	1931....Mr. E. W. K. SLADE
1918....The late Mr. E. M. NUNNELEY	1932....Mr. M. T. DAVIES
1919....Mr. F. H. PADWICK, C.B.E.	1933....Mr. B. J. GATES
1920....Mr. E. W. LANGFORD	1934....Mr. S. O. RATCLIFF
1921....Mr. R. R. ROBBINS, C.B.E.	1935....The late Mr. J. H. WAIN
1922....The late Mr. J. DONALDSON	1936....MAJOR R. H. DORMAN-SMITH, J.P., M.P.
1923....Mr. H. GERMAN, O.B.E.	
1924....Mr. T. H. RYLAND	
1925....Mr. R. R. ROBBINS, C.B.E.	1937....COL. SIR REGINALD H. DORMAN-SMITH, J.P., M.P.
1926....Mr. E. W. LANGFORD	
1927....Mr. T. BAXTER	
1928....Mr. T. WILLIAMS	1938....Mr. G. GIBBARD.
1929....The late Mr. J. GARTON.	1939....Mr. T. PEACOCK, J.P.
1930....CAPT. E. T. MORRIS	1940....Mr. T. PEACOCK, J.P.

There were NFU county branches and sub-committees to deal with all aspects of growing, marketing, etc. on behalf of the members

PAY YOUR
N.F.U. SUBSCRIPTION
BY BANKER'S ORDER

Unknown farmers, c.1915

WORKING WITH OXEN

An Ox is a bovine animal that has been castrated to increase its docility. Oxen have been used for draught purposes for many centuries, since before records began.

An engraving of 1860 HARROWING WITH OXEN

Beyond the harrows a sower broadcasts seed with the birds in attendance.

Plant your seeds in a row,
One-for pheasant, one-for crow
One to eat and one-to grow.

Farmers made the gradual change-over from oxen to horses because horses were faster and more agile.

Oxen were very hardy, travelled well over rough ground, were cheap to keep and were persistent pullers. When too old for work they could be fattened up and slaughtered for meat.

A farmer poses with an Ox. North Wales, about 1917

"THE BLACK OX HAS TRODDEN ON HIS FOOT"
Old saying, meaning misfortune or old age has come upon him.

A team of six, drawing a plough in Sussex

The last working team, of Birling Manor, East Dean, Sussex, was dispersed in 1929

Mr. Johns at Manea Cambridgeshire, about 1920

Oxen could be harnessed by yoke or by bridle and collar, that was similar to horse harness.

Several different breeds of cattle were used for work. The best ones needed to have strong shoulders and to be muscular but not fat.

Sussex Road Scene—Oxen at Work.

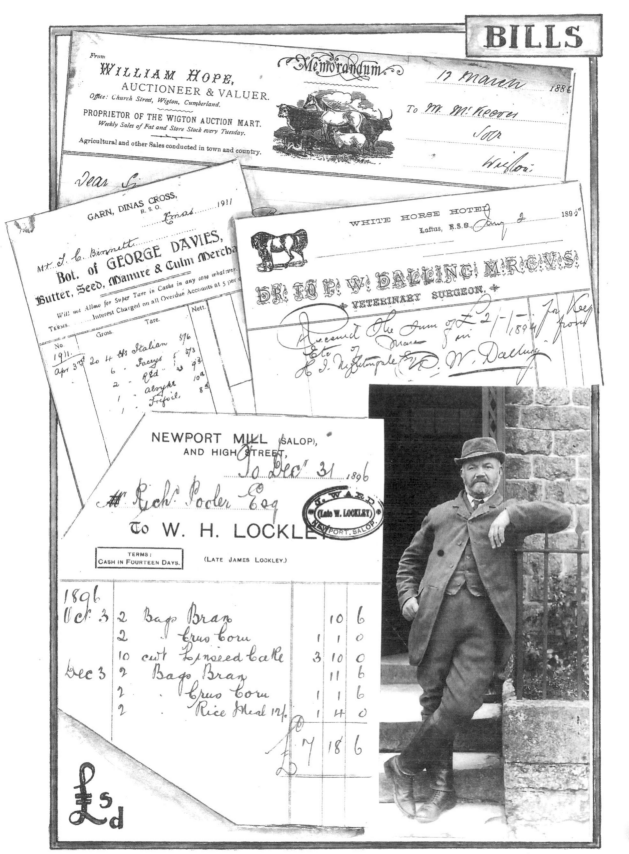

From
WILLIAM HOPE,
AUCTIONEER & VALUER.
Office: Church Street, Wigton, Cumberland.

PROPRIETOR OF THE WIGTON AUCTION MART.
Weekly Sales of Fat and Store Stock every Tuesday.

Agricultural and other Sales conducted in town and country.

Memorandum

17 March 1886

To M. McKeen

Sotr

Wigton

Dear Si...

GARN, DINAS CROSS,
R.S.O.
Xmas 1911

Mr T. C. Bennett

Bot. of GEORGE DAVIES,
Butter, Seed, Manure & Culm Mercha...

Will not Allow for Super Tare in Casks in any case whatever.
TERMS. Interest Charged on all Overdue Accounts at 5 per c...

No.	Gross.	Tare.	Nett.
1911.			
Apr 3rd	20 4 lbs Italian	5/6	
	6 " Pacey's	5/3	
	2 " Red	9d	
	1 " alsyke	10d	
	1 " Trefoil.	8d	

WHITE HORSE HOTEL
Loftus, R.S.S. Jany 2 1894

DR TO F. W. DALLING, M.R.C.V.S.
★ VETERINARY SURGEON. ★

Received the sum of £2/1/- for Keep
Etc. ... Mare from
H. J. Nightingale Esq ... F. W. Dalling

NEWPORT MILL (SALOP),
AND HIGH STREET,

To Dec 31 1896

M. Rich.d Pooler Esq

To W. H. LOCKLEY

N. WARD
(Late W. LOCKLEY)
NEWPORT. SALOP.

TERMS:		
CASH IN FOURTEEN DAYS.	(LATE JAMES LOCKLEY.)	

1896					
Oct. 3	2	Bags Bran		10	6
	2	Crus Corn	1	1	0
	10 cwt	Linseed Cake	3	10	0
Dec 3	2	Bags Bran		11	6
	2	Crus Corn	1	1	6
	2	Rice Meal 12/-	1	4	0
			£ 7	18	6

£ s d

Tithes

were paid from the 13th century and became compulsory. They provided funds for the Church of England, the amount paid being calculated on the profit made from the land. TITHE BARNS held the produce brought in by the farmers but in later times money was paid instead, as a tax on Agricultural production.

TITHE ACT, 1891.

W. H. SANDS,
LAND AGENT
AND SURVEYOR.

ESTATE OFFICE,
FARLEY,
OAKAMOOR,
NEAR STOKE-UPON-TRENT.

– 4 JUL 1922

DEAR SIR,

I beg to apply for payment of £ 13 6½ being ½ year's Tithe Rent charge due to the *Rector of Cheadle* on the 1st instant, in respect of lands in the Parish of *Cheadle.* of which you are the owner, and I shall be much obliged by your remitting me the amount on or before the *14 June* at which date the Half-yearly Audit will be held at *Town Hall Cheadle* between the hours of .... and ....

Yours faithfully,

W. H. SANDS

Mrs Barker

Throughout the centuries the people complained about having to pay the tithe, but non-payment meant imprisonment.

In WALES in 1886 there were riots in opposition to paying it and in 1890 the Military had to be called in to collect it.

1934 Some parsons in WALES sent gangs with sticks and bayonets to force the hill farmers to pay their tithes

In the 1930's the DEPRESSION bit hard. Harvests were sparse. Farmers farmed on hope. Payment became impossible for some. THE DISPUTES OVER PAYING TITHES CAME TO A HEAD.

Mr. A. E. Waddell of Ruckinge, Kent, was made bankrupt and had his cart horse, 'Old Faithful' which had given him 18 years of work, siezed for non-payment. The horse was bought by the 'Our Dumb Friends League' and returned to the farmer.

KENT. A Mrs. Andrews was said to have taken her tenth baby to the parson saying that as he claimed one tenth of everything the baby was for him. The parson gave her money to take the child away.

1933–35 Thousands refused to pay. The Church Authorities sent bailiffs to seize property: animals, machinery, furniture, etc. Farmers hid their stock or tried to defend it against the police force and sometimes from gangs of ruffians sent by the church authorities. Payments to farmers that had been owed to them by the Milk Marketing Board and the Wheat Commission were intercepted and went to the Church.

NO TITHES WITHDRAW THE TITHE BILL

PAY NO TITHE

The TITHE WAR will last another 80 YEARS

A REFORM was fixed upon in 1936 but Tithes began to cost more to collect than they brought in. The FINANCE ACT 1977 ended tithes

FARMERS' PORTRAITS

1870's. Dark coloured linen smock, bowler hat and a hazel stick, twisted in its growth by honeysuckle.

1930's. In his working clothes in Devon, with a kitten and a costrel which perhaps contains cider.

1890's. Complete with dog and stick.

1880's. The whole family dresses in their best for the photo., with two hens as well.

For to keep a farmer's spirits up
'gen things be getting low,
Theer's nothing loik Fox-huntin'
and a rattling Tally-ho!

R.Egerton-Warburton. 1853.

Following the HUNT, either on foot or on horseback was a very popular day out, encompassing everything from daring horsemanship, lords and ladies, seeing the state of other farmers' crops and unfamiliar countryside, admiring the skill of a good huntsman and hearing the local gossip.

A VERMIN SHOOT meant doing something useful and having a convivial time with neighbours from far and near. Often they were all tenants of the same estate. Rabbits were a pest that ate off everyones' crops; jays, rooks and magpies were also fair game.

On Thursday, Nov. 1st, 1917.

THE MOAT FARM,

STAPLETON,
Six Miles from Shrewsbury.

Notice of an Important Agricultural Sale.

MESSRS.

HENRY RUSSELL & SON

are favoured with instructions from Mr. Thomas Fox (who is retiring), to Sell by Auction, on the premises, the whole of his valuable

LIVE AND DEAD FARMING STOCK,
VIZ. :
A HERD OF

61 Shorthorn Cattle

Comprising 9 Grand Young Cows (close to profit), 9 Three-year-old Bullocks (in very forward condition), 3 Two-and-a-half-year old Heifers (in Calf), 21 Year-and-a-half old Cattle, and 18 Yearling and Weaned Calves.

A FLOCK OF

174 Shropshire Sheep

Viz. : 65 young Stock Ewes, 48 Yearling Ewes, 59 Ewe and Wether Lambs and 2 Rams.

3 Sows in Pig & 24 Strong Store Pigs.

A TEAM OF

12 POWERFUL WAGGON HORSES AND COLTS

Gears, a large and varied assortment of Agricultural Implements.

THE WHOLE OF THE

WINTER KEEP & UNTHRESHED GRAIN,
Comprising OATS, WHEAT, BARLEY and PEAS the produce of 65 Acres.
A few items of DAIRY VESSELS.

Luncheon Free (by Ticket) 10-30.   Sale at 11-0 a.m.

Catalogues and all particulars from the Auctioneers, 42 St. John's Chambers, Shrewsbury.

An enjoyable day out could be had in the spring at the POINT-TO-POINT races (or Steeple Chase), where there were thrills from amateur riders racing "over the sticks" on regularly hunted horses. There were drinks in the beer tent and swapping gossip, the placing of a few bets, then happily home to do the milking

O. S. & B. H.
Steeple Chases
Saturday, April 25th
1936
**Admit Bearer
to Paddock**
Price 5s. (including Tax)
Issued subject to National Hunt Rules
1587

(old Surrey and Burstow Hunt)

A FARM SALE was a social occasion, with the pleasure of inspecting the goods and being amazed at the prices they made, and often there was a free lunch as well.

Going to a SHOW and winning an award for something, if possible.
(Bronze medal presented to Wm Newman 1936)

Having a few friends round on a Sunday 1924

In 1929 there was a catastrophic crash on the Stock Market and a World wide DEPRESSION.

The **1930's** were bad years for farming in most districts. When a tenant left a farm, the landlord had difficulty letting it.

Although rents were cheap, money was scarce and, at times, some farmers were reduced to selling personal belongings to pay the weekly wages of their men

Greenbank Farm, Cumbria, with Blencathra in the background.

The author's father, Frederick Raybould, had plenty of farms to choose from when he rented his first farm in 1931. He took Falcon Farm at Enville, Staffordshire, 100 acres.
He employed one boy. Like others in a similar situation he and his family lived frugally, working very hard, managing to meet their bills, eating their own produce most of the time, and wearing their clothes until they fell to pieces.

Neither landlords nor farmers had money to repair buildings or to buy new equipment and the tractors that were now becoming available.

In areas where the depression was not so pronounced, such as Norfolk, farmers of several hundred acres began to mechanise.

A good root crop in 1933

• SHOWS • The ROYAL AGRICULTURAL SOCIETY was

founded in 1838 and held an Annual Show. There were prizes for "Best Brood Mare", "Cart Mare", "Colt", etc. and for other animals. County Societies were then formed and held their own shows.

Towards the end of the century horses being judged for beauty and conformation were decked with ribbons, raffia and wheat straw plaited into the mane and tail. The plaiting styles varied according to the locality and breed of horse. Men with artistic tendencies and decorating skills were in demand. They could improve a horse's chances in the ring by, for instance, making a thin neck appear thicker, according to the mane decoration.

"My Dad, at Camp Farm, near Lichfield, decided to enter our particularly good-looking Shire mare, called Brown, in a show. He hired a skilled man to decorate her mane and tail. We thought she looked splendid in her orange and blue finery and were disappointed that she didn't actually win anything, although she attracted many admiring remarks. I was a small girl and I hoped that the ribbons would fall to me afterwards but the hired decorator granted me only two from her tail; the others he took away to use again."

the Author.

• SALES •

With the introduction of railways, giving easier transport, auction sales became popular. Horses were walked, sent by train or, later on, delivered by motor lorry ⤳

THE SHROPSHIRE MONTHLY HORSE SALE,
RAVEN REPOSITORY,
SHREWSBURY. Mch 5 1919

SALES THE LAST FRIDAY AND SATURDAY IN EACH MONTH.

No Dealing transacted by any Member of the Firm, who act solely as Agents between Sellers and Buyers.

m the exors of the late R J Davies Esq herefort

In Account with HALL, WATERIDGE & OWEN,
AUCTIONEERS & VALUERS, HIGH STREET, SHREWSBURY.
ALSO AT WELLINGTON, WEM, AND OSWESTRY.

All Communications to be addressed to High Street, Shrewsbury.

PLEASE NOTE—Entries Close Saturday, August 17th, 1929
ENTRY FORM for One Animal
AUTUMN
SALE OF SUFFOLK HORSES
AT IPSWICH,
On THURSDAY, September 12th, 1929
Under the auspices of the Suffolk Horse Society,
to include
Fillies, Foals, Stallions, and Geldings

THE SECOND WORLD WAR 1939~1945

At a Cattle Market

Trilby hats, caps and a bowler (now going out of fashion), with Macintoshes over suits are farmers' choice.

DIG
FOR
VICTORY

As in the First World War, imports from abroad became scarce. The farmers had to produce enough to feed the British population.

The government was again obliged to intervene by setting up WAR AGRICULTURAL COMMITTEES similar to those of 1916, in order to persuade and force farmers to plough up grassland and to grow arable crops.

Local committee men directed farmers as to what they must grow, but, although farmers were in sympathy with the government's aim of increasing the number of acres that had to be planted, there was often unco-operation with the War Ag. men. Sometimes these were inexperienced, unsympathetic or gave bad advice. They were also feared, for they had powers to evict (without right of appeal) any farmer who was unwilling or unable to carry out orders.

From a letter by an anonymous farmer's son of Sutton-on-the-Forest, Yorks.

"My own father cried when he was ordered to plough up his beloved meadowlands and pull out hedges, etc.....We sowed grain...but the wireworm and the leatherjacket grubbed most of it off. A smartly dressed man appeared in a taxi and said sow a mixture of bran and paris green on, that will stop them, but it nearly choked us, we had no masks... I always suspected they [the War Ag. men] carried a whip about their person because the farmers were scared of them".

Despite being beset with many difficulties, with shortages, lack of labour and equipment, "red tape" and disputes, the PLOUGH UP CAMPAIGN was successful. Between 1939 - 1944 arable crops increased from 12,900,000 acres to 19,400,000 acres, with the amount of home-grown food increased by over 70%

Not only did food for humans become scarce and it was rationed during the War but animal foodstuffs were in very short supply as well.

Pigs, good feeders, cheap, ..c.p.—Particulars, Walter Giddings, 30, St. Michael's, Bedford.

Pigman for Broadway herd of ped. Essex pigs.— A. B. Williams, West End, Broadway, Worcs.

TUESDAY, JAN. 12 (12 noon), in the Cattle Market, READING, 1942
130 BREEDING PIGS
comprising pure-bred and unregistered WESSEX SADDLEBACKS, LARGE WHITES, LARGE BLACKS, etc., and including served gilts, maiden gilts and 30 young boars.

THE WAR-TIME PIG
Gloster Old Spots
Good Grazers :: Quick Feeders
Heavy Weights :: Splendid Quality
Send for particulars
The Secretary
36 BALDWIN STREET, BRISTOL

Experienced Pigman for Wessex Herd.—Brooks- bank, Sandrock Farm, Tickhill, Doncaster.

Sleeping Gloucester Old Spots.

Just before the War began FREDERIC BURKE had taken a small holding of 13 acres next door to his father's holding of 25 acres, near Aldridge in Staffordshire. He specialised in pigs, poultry and store cattle.

"We had to conform to the War Agricultural Committee and plough 12 of the 13 acres and grow potatoes and oats.

Poultry and pig rations were based on ⅛th of the total recorded in the last Ministry of Agriculture and Fisheries' returns. What a body blow this was!

We were forced to obtain processed waste from a Birmingham factory canteen, known as "Tottenham Puddings", and the smell was terrible! These puddings also contained cutlery, broken glass, bones, and quite a few other obnoxious things. As you may imagine the vet did quite well!! The poultry had "dried waste", which had to be supplemented with rolled oats.

Of course rationing went on into the fifties but we were able to buy powdered skim milk imported from New Zealand, and surplus bread and cakes from the Birmingham Co-op Bakery, which we stored in a Nissan Hut. All these "goodies" attracted both rats and the boy who worked for me! One would pick up a perfectly shaped loaf to find it had been hollowed out by hungry rats! However the pigs thrived on their diet and produced wonderful top grade bacon".

F. Burke.

The last load of hay attracts visitors in the late 1930's

Women workers returning from the fields. The cross-over apron was every-day wear for women all over the country in the 1930's – 40's.

Ashwell, Rutland

The horse wears ear-caps to ward off flies. Sometimes these were used for decoration. They were particulary popular for canal -boat horses.

Field workers were still in short supply after the war. These girls are helping out at Ashwell Voluntary Agricultural Camp in 1948, where they went partly to work (for very low payment) and partly for a holiday from their regular office jobs.

THE ARCHERS

1950

After the Second World War **GODFREY BASELEY**, a radio executive in the Midlands, was inspired to start a programme designed to provide farmers with information on modern agricultural trends. This programme was set in a fictional village and centred upon a farming family called "THE ARCHERS." He found the title by putting the names of acquaintances who had suitable sounding names into a hat. The name "**DAN ARCHER**" was drawn out and Dan became a founding character.

Godfrey Baseley
1904~1993

Godfrey Baseley had known the Archer family since 1914, when they had moved from Derbyshire to Rowney Green, the village up the hill above Alvechurch, where Baseley was the son of the butcher. He and Dan Archer were the same age and they attended Alvechurch school. For a few years the Archers lived in an old farm-house, called "The Storrige" but later on moved to a farm which had a terraced garden, pond and tennis court in Rowney Green village.

Daniel Archer, junior
1904~1973

Dan's father, also called Daniel, took in farm pupils and he was a superb horseman. There were five children in the family: Nancy, Dan, Marjorie, Clare and Betty. Visitors were always welcome. They were a social family and enjoyed having parties. In 1923 they left Rowney Green for Gloucestershire but stayed in touch with villagers.

Daniel Archer, senior
1876~1929

Dan joined the Metropolitan Police Force and he spent the war years in London. He kept pigs at the police station, collecting pig swill from the fashionable houses and restaurants in Park Lane. Eventually he returned to the Birmingham area. He died in 1973 and was buried at Beoley, just a few miles away from Rowney Green and Alvechurch.

47

Farmers' Wives and Daughters

A wife was almost a necessity for a farmer.

Up with the birds in the morning —
The dew-drops glow like a precious gem;
Beautiful tints in the skies are dawning,
But she's never a moment to look at them.
The men are wanting their breakfast early;
She must not linger, she must not wait,
For words that are sharp and looks that
              are surly
Are what men give when meals are late.

To glorious colour the clouds are turning
If she would but look over hills and trees;
But here are the dishes and here is the
              churning
Those things must always yield to these.
The world is filled with the wine of beauty
If she could but pause and drink it in;
But pleasure, she says, must wait for duty—
Neglected work is committed sin.

They do not know that the heart within her
Hungers for beauty and things sublime;
They only know that they want their dinner—
Plenty of it — and "just in time".
And after the sweeping and churning
              and baking;
And dinner dishes are all put by,
She sits and sews, though her head is aching,
'Till time for supper and "chores" draws nigh.

from "The Farmer's Wife". Anonymous.

from a carte-de-visite photograph, about 1865

The farmer's wife's life revolved around bringing up the children, organising the housework and the indoor servants, if any were kept, and preparing, cooking and serving meals, including extra meals for hired men. She preserved and bottled fruit and vegetables, made pickles, chutney and jam, did the laundry, the ironing and mending, made clothes and knitted socks, etc. Outside, her special responsibility was for the poultry and the dairy work — she churned butter and made cream. When labour was short she helped in the fields,

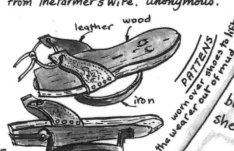

leather   wood

PATTENS
worn over shoes to lift the wearer out of mud.

iron

THE UNDERSIDE

48

The FARMER'S WIFE, or a grown-up DAUGHTER who could run the house, was indispensable. Without her work the farm could not flourish. She had been brought up to expect a hard and busy life and she did not question it. When she bore children she rested for a day or two, often assisted by a female relation. After the birth of her first child, farmers frequently addressed their wives as "Mother". Going to market made a small holiday, or she might get away for two or three days to stay with a relation.

A Suffolk woman in about 1870. From a carte de visite by W S Spanton Bury St Edmonds

Feeding the fowl in the rickyard. Care of the poultry was a traditional task for the farmer's wife, from which she could make some pin money for herself.

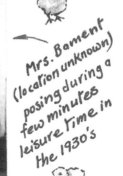

Mrs. Bament (location unknown) posing during a few minutes leisure time in the 1930's

49

FARMERS' DAUGHTERS usually had an easier life than their brothers. They were brought up to help in the house, learning from their mothers the tasks that would be useful to them when they themselves married. When it came to horses and hunting, women, even in pre-emancipated times, managed to participate alongside men. Indulgent fathers bought ponies for their daughters and taught them to ride.

1940's, wearing a shirt and jodhpurs.

Photographed in Ipswich by Walter A. Smith, in the 1870's, this young woman wears a simple riding habit with a brooch at the neck, earrings and what appears to be a fur hat.

In the 1920's this woman is casually dressed for riding, in breeches worn with knee socks and a jumper. Her hair is tied back with a wide ribbon under a bowler hat

• THE PONY CLUB •

Founded in 1929 to encourage young people to ride and to enjoy sport connected with horses. Children and their ponies met to receive instruction on improving their riding skills and in the care of their horses.
Members: under age 17
Associate Members: age 17-21

Children under instruction, Bedfordshire, early 1930's

Farmers' Sons

JOSEPH GWYER was born in 1835 in Redlench, near Salisbury. He was 8 years old when his mother died, leaving his father with eight children. Joseph was sent to remote Lodge Farm, his grandmother's farm, which was managed by his uncle.

"The shire is Wilts, suffice to state
With Lords and Ladies fair,
The highest spire and stones so great,
Moonrakers everywhere."

"My uncle was intent upon my being brought up in an industrious way: he therefore made me do as much for a lad, as was necessary, and I have thought a great deal too much. I attended the British School at Downton, a town about two miles distant from the farm----"

"Before I went to school I had to milk the cows and drive them to the meadow, which was about a mile from the farm, and then get to school at nine o'clock in the morning. I left school at half past three o'clock, took the cows from the meadow, milked, and often had to mind them in the evening, so that with learning and work my young mind and body were pretty well taxed, and, as the old adage says, all work and no play made Joe a dull boy---"

"On Saturdays and holidays I often used to act as ploughboy, and occasionally my thick head had a clod thrown at it, as the ploughman used to say he would as soon have an old maid out of the workhouse to drive the plough. On Sundays the cows had to be attended to in a similar way. I had to go to the Wesleyan Sunday School at Downton at nine in the morning. My uncle was a class leader at this chapel."

"I left my home at seventeen,
Great London town to see.
I thought the streets were paved with gold
But cold they were to me."

Joseph went to London in 1852 to visit another uncle and he stayed on. By the 1870's he was a self-employed Potato Salesman, who published his own verses and travelled by horse-drawn van in a 12 mile radius of Penge, Surrey

"In Ivy Cottage, Hawthorne Grove,
Your humble servant dwell
I traffic not in gold or gems
But to the public sell —

Potatoes, which stand next to bread,
The staff of life to man,
So if the chance presents itself
Buy of me if you can."

Generally speaking, farmers did not believe in spending money to educate their sons more than was lawfully necessary. If the boys were to become farmers then the fathers thought they could teach them all they needed to know on the farm itself. The boys left school at the current minimum leaving age.

> THREE THINGS ARE NOT TO BE TRUSTED: A COW'S HORN, A DOG'S TOOTH AND A HORSE'S HOOF.

Richard Jefferies, writing in 1880, said of a farmer's son: "He has worked exceedingly hard in his life time. In his youth, though his family were then well to-do, he was not permitted to lounge about in idleness, but had to work hard in the fields... Trudging to and from the neighbouring country town, in wind, in wet and in snow to school, his letters were thrashed into him. In holiday time he went to work —"

Most farmers' sons led similar lives right through the decades, working as unpaid labourers for their fathers until well into adulthood, sometimes not managing to escape parental authority until their fathers died.

OFF TO WORK.

Ploughboy or Farmer's Son, the work was the same.

A boy in charge of a Middle White Boar (bred from 1882 for the pork trade), He was called Rufford Primrose, the property of H. Sykes of Copley House, Dogley, Yorks 1905

52

Farmers' Children had the privileges of riding and shooting when time permitted

1924
Frank and Mary Yeomans with Peggy, the pony, at "Birchacres", Beoley Warwickshire. Their father, Albert, sadly died at age 66 after falling from a ladder whilst picking apples

A jolly smile from a girl with her brothers, one holding a pet hen, in about 1930

The Complete Ratcatcher, about 1910

⚬ YOUNG FARMERS' CLUB ⚬

The National Federation of Young Farmers' Clubs was set up in 1932 for young people between the ages of 10 and 25. The idea was that they should meet together to increase their knowledge and appreciation of rural life. with a varied programme of educational, social and recreational activities, as well as practical agricultural activities. Clubs were formed in many areas, the members being drawn from young people in all walks of life

HORSEMEN

He starts, and ever thoughtful of his team,
Along the glittering snow, a feeble gleam
Shoots from his lantern, as he yawning goes
To add fresh comforts to their night's repose;
Diffusing fragrance as their food he moves,
And pats the jolly sides of those he loves.

Robert Bloomfield - 1766-1823

Men who worked with horses were called by different names according to the area:
PLOUGHMAN = North Eastern Area, HORSEMAN = Northwest, Southwest, East Anglia
WAGONER = the greater part of England and Wales
CARTER = southern England

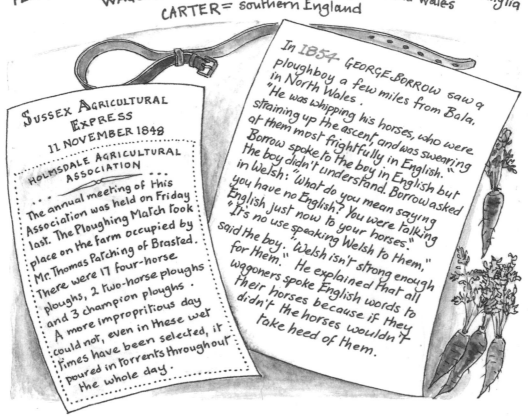

SUSSEX AGRICULTURAL
EXPRESS
11 NOVEMBER 1848

HOLMSDALE AGRICULTURAL
ASSOCIATION

... annual meeting of this
Association was held on Friday
last. The Ploughing Match took
place on the farm occupied by
Mr. Thomas Patching of Brasted.
There were 17 four-horse
ploughs, 2 two-horse ploughs
and 3 champion ploughs.
A more impropritious day
could not, even in these wet
times have been selected, it
poured in torrents throughout
the whole day.

In 1854 GEORGE BORROW saw a
ploughboy a few miles from Bala,
in North Wales.
"He was whipping his horses, who were
straining up the ascent, and was swearing
at them most frightfully in English."
Borrow spoke to the boy in English but
the boy didn't understand. Borrow asked
in Welsh: "What do you mean saying
you have no English? You were talking
English just now to your horses."
"It's no use speaking Welsh to them,"
said the boy. "Welsh isn't strong enough
for them." He explained that all
wagoners spoke English words to
their horses because if they
didn't the horses wouldn't
take heed of them.

The **HEAD HORSEMAN,** or FOREMAN on a large farm was on a par in the farm hierarchy with the Shepherd. They were both trusted to work independently and to make their own decisions. The Head Horseman was in command of the other horsemen on the farm.

He began work at 5 a.m, feeding the horses, so that they would have time to digest their food before starting work. The other men arrived at 6 a.m. He also fed the horses on Sundays when the others had a day off.

Before setting off for work the horses were groomed and their tails braided. Most draught horses' tails were docked to prevent them from being caught up in harness or machinery, but there was still enough hair to plait with a wisp of straw, and to be twisted up neatly into a particular style.

"I remember that every morning my Dad selected a wisp of straw, (just a few stalks), and he plaited up the straw with the tail hair. In the evening, whilst the horses munched on their bran and chaff, he undid them again, running his fingers through the hair to comb it out. The loosening of the tails signified the end of the day's toil for the horses, freedom and rest." The Author.

~ about 1900 ~
wearing thigh-length
buckled gaiters, or "knee buskins"

The HEAD MAN took pride in the appearance of his horses and he often gave them extra grooming in his own time, as well as acquiring more food for them. He obtained ingredients that would improve their condition and make their coats shine. He diligently polished harness and brasses, which often belonged to him and not to the farmer who employed him.

THE TEAM

SIX HORSES could be cared for by ONE MAN and A BOY but a large farm needed more horses to work the land, together with more men.

HEAD HORSEMAN, WAGONER or CARTER or FOREMAN

SECOND HORSEMAN

THIRD HORSEMAN or WAGONER'S LAD

then FOURTH, etc, down to the:

LEAST LAD or PLOUGHBOY, the newest to the team

different terms were used in different districts

~ drawn from a faded photograph ~

A TEAM with the LEAST LAD second from the right, probably in YORKSHIRE

In Yorkshire the men were usually unmarried and lived in at the farm. When there were several of them they slept in dormitories, with a box each to contain their belongings. Their meals were provided.

They took pride in their skill and in the horses, and the men cared for them as if they themselves owned them.

The HEAD HORSEMAN took the lead in everything. He and his horses headed the procession to the fields and back again in the evening. He sat down first for his meals, etc.

The LEAST LAD had the oldest horses and was last for everything but, apart from carrying heavy sacks, he had to keep up with the others.

If there was a bath he washed when they had finished, in the same water used by all, and he dried himself on the wet towel that they had used.

Secret Potions
and MYSTERIOUS POWERS

A few horsemen seemed to have powers over horses which mystified their co-workers. There was said to be a "brotherhood" whose members had a "knowledge", not only a recollection of pedigrees, (at that time not written down), but of remedies for complaints, and of potions and powders for aiding control and condition. They did not like to part with their knowledge.

CONTROL. A vicious horse could be made docile, or a horse could be jaded, or prevented from moving a step forwards, or it could be drawn towards and attracted to the horseman. The power to control the animal in this way relied upon various secret mixtures which repelled or attracted the horse by its sense of smell.

CONDITION To keep the horses in superb condition, with shining coats, powders were given to encourage them to eat well. Horsemen concocted their own receipts using various oils and substances from the chemist. Some gave poisonous chemicals, such as small quantities of arsenic or antimony, which helped to keep horses fat and sleek.

Charm for an Injured Horse

Our Lord forth raide
His foal's foot slade,
Our Lord down-lighted,
His foal's foot righted,
Saying "flesh to flesh,
blood to blood,
and bane to bane."
In our Lord His name.

(raide=rode, bane=bone)

JUNIPER
AGRIMONY
FEVERFEW
DRAGON'S BLOOD
FENUGREEK
MINT

During the 1914-18 WAR so many men and horses were killed in the fighting that it is likely most of their secrets died with them.

CLOTHES

Best Wear c.1895

On SUNDAYS, and for SPECIAL OCCASIONS, horsemen liked to dress distinctively, especially when they took pride in their positions as HEAD or SECOND horseman.

Red spotted muffler wound twice round the neck and tied at the side.

Fustian/velvet-fronted waist-coat with watch-chain showing.

Corduroy, moleskin or thick woollen jacket, fancy stitching at cuffs and shoulders, with, perhaps, a velvet collar.

Front-fall corduroy trousers lined with flannelette, with bell-bottoms that were sometimes inlet with a panel of black velvet or split at the bottoms. Pearl buttons decorated the sides of the trousers.

Work Wear c.1910

Fustian body and calico-sleeved waist-coat — very popular with working men of all kinds

Corduroy trousers

Lincolnshire "fenners" liked to wear bright blue cords with many pearl buttons decorating breeches and leggings. In Yorkshire jackets, worn open, might have two or three inches of brass chain as a fastening across the chest.

MOTHER-OF-PEARL BUTTONS

an elaborate buckle-like button, with diamanté and brass

thick, wavy, pearl with brass shank behind

cuff link

Clothes were usually made by local tailors who walked or bicycled to the farms or took a room at an inn where they took orders and measured the customers.

THE DINNER HOUR • Etching by Joseph Benwell Clarke (c.1880)

The horsemen worked eleven hours a day, six days a week. Some took an hour's break at noon for dinner time, either in the stable if the day's work was not far from the farm buildings or, otherwise, out in the field, where they gave the horses some hay.

At some farms they worked until three in the afternoon with short breaks for breakfast, (nineses), and a snack later on, (elevenses). After work they returned to the stable, fed the horses, had their own dinner at four, then groomed the horses, laid down straw for their bedding, and prepared the horses' bait ready for next morning

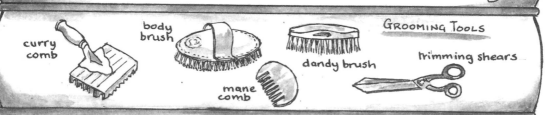

GROOMING TOOLS

curry comb

body brush

mane comb

dandy brush

trimming shears

59

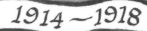

In the FIRST WORLD WAR horses from all over the country were commandeered for the war effort. They were assembled on village greens and in town squares where buyers from the British Army made compulsory purchases. All types of horses: heavy for haulage and light for riding, were sent abroad to face terrible conditions and painful deaths.

500,000 horses were killed in the war.

A few returned home afterwards but they were often shell-shocked, terrified of loud noises, or even of someone wearing a soldier's uniform. Some were sold off at the end of the war in the country where they had been fighting, for work if they were fit enough, or for meat.

Farmers were left with only brood mares and very young horses to till the land. Many of the experienced horsemen had gone to the war and men who were skilled with stallions and in-foal mares were scarce on the farms.

1,000,000 men died in the war

After 1919, with the war over, a law reduced the farm workers' and the horsemens' hours to 9 on Mondays to Fridays, with work finishing at noon on Saturdays

A plough team. The horses wear open bridles (no blinkers) in the Scottish style.

60

— Sitting Sideways —
at The Old Malthouse, Gomshall, Surrey

from "Going Home Together"
(an anonymous horseman of the 1st World War thinks of the lads and their horses)

Old 'Captain', 'Boxer', and 'Traveller'. I see them all so plain,
With tasselled ear caps nodding along a leafy lane,
There's a bird somewhere calling and swallows flying low,
And the lads sitting sideways and singing as they go.

Well, gone is many a lad now, and many a horse gone too,
Of all the lads and horses in those fields I knew,
Like Dick that fell at Givenchy, and 'Prince' beside the guns
On that red road of glory a mile or two from Mons......

Dead lads and shadowy horses, I see them just the same,
I see them and I know them and name them each by name,
Going down to quiet waters when all the west's aglow
And the lads sitting sideways and singing as they go.

Home lads, home, with the sunset in their faces,
Home lads, home, in the quiet and happy places.
Oh, there's rest for horse and man when the long day is done,
And they go home together at the setting of the sun.

61

A plough boy cuts the first furrow across a field. All other furrows would be parallel to it, so it was important that it was straight.

A brass "face piece", worn on the horse's forehead

or on a breast strap, running from collar to girth.

SUNDAYS were days of rest

Apart from feeding the horses there was no work on Sundays and the men could do as they wished. Occasionally an employer might insist that they went to church in the morning.

On Sundays the horseman might stroll along the lanes to look critically at the neighbours' fields, or visit a friend at another farm and inspect the horses that he cared for. If the village were near he might go to visit other horse lads there, or if his family lived within reach he could spend the day at home.

Many horsemen sat sideways when riding to and from the fields. It took practice and agility to mount in this way, by gripping the harness and mane with both hands while facing the horse, then leaping upwards and twisting, to land facing outwards.

Fly terret, with swinging disc, attached to the top of the bridle, between the ears.

HORSE DECORATION

Brass Fly terret of the Scottish style, with a spike to fit into the top of the collar

BRASS began to be used on heavy horse harness towards the close of the 1700's. It was not until about 1870 that brasses became fashionable wear for horses, and farmers and wagoners could afford them. By 1920 most horses went out to work with some brass decorating the harness.

The HORSEMAN loved to show off his horses. Before a journey into town with his team he polished the harness and brasses. He took pride in the whole turn-out

RIBBONS AND FLOWERS, as well as brasses, decked the horses for special occasions, such as May Day Parades, Ploughing Matches, Harvest Festival, or a Sunday School outing when the farm wagon was used for transport. Flowers were real or made from paper, and satin rosettes, woollen tassels and fringes were used as well. Some shows held competitions for the best decorated horse.

TOM CLARKE, about 1930, location unknown. His horse wears cart harness and he may have been entered in a show for Best Decorated Horse. The horse wears a wire hoop, with flowers attached, fixed over the collar, and a small Union Flag flying. There are woollen fringes round the haunches, "standards" on saddle and crupper, and ribbon wound round the breeching and noseband; in fact he wears a real assortment! Tom and his family probably made most of the decorations themselves.

SHOWS, held for judging the conformation and beauty of the horses, required a different and more formal style of decoration. Apart from a bridle no harness was worn, so decoration was confined to ribbons, plaits and "standards" in the mane and tail.

The Ploughing Match

After the end of harvest ploughing matches began, designed to test the skill of all who believed that they could plough a furrow to perfection. From September through to November horses were decked up, beer tents were erected and hopeful plough teams gathered on stubble fields. Each competitor ploughed half an acre with his horses (a five-mile stretch), with an audience of critical farmers and country people. At the end of the day the work was judged.

An unknown ploughman of the 1920's with his medals and the PLOUGHING CHAMPIONSHIP CUP which had been awarded by Mr R. Garden. Unfortunately other inscriptions on the cup cannot be deciphered.

A certificate awarded by WEST GRINSTEAD, (West Sussex) PLOUGHING SOCIETY to H. Muggeridge in September 1931 (First Prize and Cup in Class 5)

Ploughing Society
Certificate of Merit
Awarded to
WON WITH RANSOMES' PLOUGH.

PRESENTED BY
Ransomes Sims & Jefferies Limited
IPSWICH AND GRANTHAM

An early tractor with three wheels pulling a binder in a harvest field →

Two horses were needed to plough one furrow, three sometimes ploughed a double furrow, which is here effortlessly ploughed using a tractor.

TRACTORS

began to be used more frequently, when they could be obtained, during the Second World War and they signalled the end of the heavy horse and of the horseman on the land.

By 1947-48 mechanisation took over completely. As a consequence thousands upon thousands of heavy horses were slaughtered. Shires, Clydesdales and Suffolks, as well as Percherons, (introduced from France after 1918) became almost extinct, along with the skills of the men who worked and understood them.

from THE TEAM-MAN'S LAMENT
Charles L. Smith (of Norwich) 1947

That earn't no good sayin' "Woosh"
Nor yit "Cubbear" to a tractor,
That hearn't got a nice sorft nose
Like welvet
What snubble up agin yer pocket
Fer a napple or a bit o' sweet.

65

The Stallion Man

As it was impractical for mares to travel long distances to be mated with a chosen stallion, the stallion was walked to his mares by his LEADER, MAN, GROOM or WALKER

The breeding of cart-horses was not recorded until stud-books began: 1877-1880. Before then the horses of the British Isles were of many different types and qualities.

A Stallion Man with "England's Glory". 1859.

The STALLION MAN

was probably first employed in the 1700's when it was realised that the horse did not need to remain in a paddock with the mare for several days but need only meet her briefly when she was in season.

In the early days the horse and groom made overnight stops at Inns as they toured the area visiting mares. The grooms had a reputation for drinking. As Societies with subscribing members developed, many overnight stops were made at farms. The man was accommodated in a spare room and the horse in the best stable.

As interest in selective breeding grew, gentlemen and wealthy farmers began to set up studs to produce strong draught horses. The sires were paraded at fairs and shows where farmers who owned well-bred, approved mares, could select a mate for them.

The GROOM'S JOB

was to see that his horse was well turned out, that he served the mares efficiently and safely in suitable premises, and that the horse himself was not likely to be injured by a mare who objected to the proceedings. The stallion himself was sometimes vicious and often needed careful handling. He wanted for nothing, whatever his character.

A good stallion was very valuable. In 1891 a promising 2-year old could fetch 1000 guineas, a champion show prize-winner could command 2,500 guineas (£2,625)

66

~ THE HEAVY HORSE BREEDS ~

The Suffolk Punch
(stud book from 1877)

The Clydesdale
(stud book from 1878)

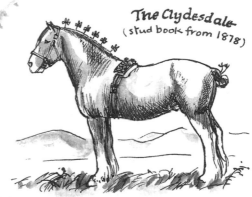

Of ancient origin and always a chestnut/sorrel colour. It possesses immense hauling strength. Used mainly in Suffolk and East Anglia

Believed to have originated in the Clyde valley and crossed with Flemish and Shire blood. It is an excellent farm horse and was extensively used in Scotland and in northern England

THE TRAVELLING SEASON FOR THE STALLION and his MAN BEGAN ON 1ST APRIL AND CONTINUED INTO THE SUMMER

Mares are receptive to the horse at intervals of about 21 days throughout February to July

The Shire
(stud book from 1880)

Believed to have originated in the Leicester/Warwick area in the 1700's as large black horses capable of great strength. It was used widely on farms and in town for haulage work

When travelling, the groom plaited up the horse's tail every morning, including one or two ribbons. He plaited the mane and sometimes added a ribbon, but these were usually kept for shows.

They walked up to 15 miles a day, which kept them both fit, stopping off at farms, where the stallion served the mares who awaited him.

SEASON 1927.

THE SHIRE STALLION

'ROYAL HERO'

The Property of M. J. Roberts and D. Rees, Tynyparc, Faerdref, Corwen, Merioneth.

FOALED 1920.   HEIGHT—16.2 HANDS.

COLOUR—DARK BAY.

Holds the Ministry of Agriculture and Fisheries Certificate.

ROUTE.

MONDAY—Cynwyd 11 a.m.; Henguc: Isa ? p.m.

TUESDAY & WEDNESDAY—Home.

THURSDAY—Caletthr 10 a.m.; Tyisa Tre Rhiwaedog 12 a.m.; Llangower 3 p.m.; Llanuwchllyn for the night.

FRIDAY—Leave Goat Hotel 10 a.m., via Parc and Llanycil, King's Head, Bala, 1-30 p.m.; Tynddol Isa, Frongoch, 3-30 p.m.; Tyucha, Ciltalgarth for the night.

SATURDAY—Leave Tyucha 10 a.m.; Penncha'rllan, Llanfor, 1 p.m.; Tynddol, Llandderfel, 3 p.m. Home for the night.

FEE 30/-.   GROOM'S FEE 2/6.

Groom's Fee to be paid first time of serving.

All Mares to be served at Owner's Risk but every care will be taken.

11 March 1912 · FARMER AND STOCKBREEDER

WANTED. Steady reliable Man to travel Shire stallion for season.
Apply–W.H.Neale, Shustoke. Coleshill, Birmingham.

WANTED. Groom to look after 2 Shire stallions and travel.
Apply – G. Wright, Damask Farm, Warminster.

A stud card which the groom handed out to farmers to show the route he would take

67

The STALLION GROOMS were smartly turned out, in good quality breeches and polished boots and leggings. They carried very little with them when walking: some clean detachable collars to freshen up the shirt, socks, boot-polish, soap and towel and maybe a paperback book. For the horse, who carried the pack, were grooming tools, some ribbons and raffia.

MANE DECORATION FOR SHOWING

GREY SPARK, the beautiful dapple-grey Shire that escaped from his loose box in the middle of the night in 1941, when visiting my father's farm near Lichfield. (the author)

THE RESULT: a promising colt (in this case a Clydesdale) decked with pom poms in about 1910

68

THE BLACKSMITH

The Smith's main tools were the fire and its bellows, his anvil, his vice and innumerable hammers, tongs, pincers, parers, punches, rasps, knives, etc.

ANVIL of wrought iron or mild steel, set onto an oak or elm BLOCK with vertical grain, which gave the anvil "spring" when struck.

Before the advent of the Veterinary Surgeon country people went to the FARRIER for advice when their animals were ill. They were often recommended potions and remedies that were strange and unsuccessful. In particular the FARRIER dealt with horses and this included shoeing them. The BLACKSMITH shod them too, but did not usually dispense cures.

During the 1800's many Societies and Companies of both FARRIERS and BLACK-SMITHS were formed. By the end of the century they were amalgamating. As scientific knowledge increased there were, by 1905, several universities teaching veterinary science.

from a postcard

By the nature of their work FARRIERS/BLACKSMITHS gained a sound knowledge of horses and their ailments. They continued to be consulted as the majority of folk could not afford vets' fees and they were suspicious of modern remedies.

The **BLACKSMITH** had to be physically strong. He was at risk of accidents from wrestling with difficult horses that weighed up to a ton. He needed to be a patient man, not only in handling fractious and kicking horses, but sometimes in dealing with their owners too, who might be ignorant, opinionated or unwilling to pay their bills.

A good smith could work wonders with an apparently lame horse, or one with a poor action, by creating shoes that would ease the foot or alter the gait. Many horses were not comfortable because their shoes did not suit them.

The smith's main occupation was shoeing but he was called upon to do various repairs to machinery, tools, gates, etc.

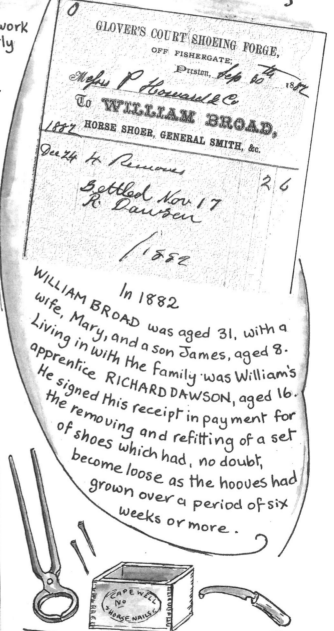

GLOVER'S COURT SHOEING FORGE,
OFF FISHERGATE;
Preston, Sep 30th 1882

Messrs P Howard & Co

To **WILLIAM BROAD,**
HORSE SHOER, GENERAL SMITH, &c.

1882

Dec 24   4 Removes   2 6

Settled Nov 17
R Dawson

/1882

In 1882 WILLIAM BROAD was aged 31, with a wife, Mary, and a son James, aged 8. Living in with the family was William's apprentice RICHARD DAWSON, aged 16. He signed this receipt in payment for the removing and refitting of a set of shoes which had, no doubt, become loose as the hooves had grown over a period of six weeks or more.

CAPEWELL No 5 HORSE NAILS

The smith always wore a leather apron, split partway up. Sometimes a fringe was cut along the bottom.

The **BLACKSMITH'S SHOP**, with the fire in its forge and the pungent smell of burning hoof, was an attractive place to catch up with local gossip whilst waiting for the horse to be shod.

The SHOP itself was divided into two rooms or areas: the Shoeing Shed, or Penthouse, where the horses were fitted with their shoes, and the Forge where the fire, its bellows, the anvil, vice and the tools were kept. Here the smith heated the iron bars, bent and fashioned them into horse shoes, and then carried them back and forth between forge and shed as he heated and hammered, adjusting them to fit the hooves.

Smithy at NORTH CURRY, SOMERSET, with The White Hart in the background.
about 1912

Bob Duke	Charles Denman	Thomas Duke	Jesse Duke	George Lock
Blacksmith's Apprentice	born 1850 Agricultural Labourer	born 1867	born 1872 BLACKSMITH	born 1847 former Gardener and father of the publican

Old Riddle.

What shoemaker makes shoes without leather,
With all the four elements put together?
Fire and water, earth and air,
Every customer has two pair

"Who would have prophesied twenty years ago that before the expiration of the next twenty years there would be Horse Shoeing Schools on wheels travelling about the country!"

'Son of the Soil' Jan. 1894

The blacksmith (in waistcoat) holds the red hot metal and beats it with a small hammer, whilst the striker, with a large hammer, beats alternately to him, to forge an iron bar into a thinner section. Sparks fly

A SUSSEX smith, GAIUS CARLEY, began his career early in the 1900's, when he was 14 years old. He had to keep the forge tidy, to learn the sizes of nuts and bolts, stocks and dies and the uses for all the tools. He had to drill and punch holes in iron and learn the tricky art of the fire: how to control it with the bellows and how to make the heat and the size of the fire suitable for different jobs.

One of his tasks, which he did not like to do, was wielding the sledge-hammer. One of his early jobs was to remove the old worn shoes from horses. "Get under him, he won't hurt you," the boss would say to the hesitant boy

HORSE SHOE ENTRANCES

A fine timber entrance to a sturdy building at Penshurst. KENT

A forbidding-looking forge at Machynlleth, WALES, built in brick and stone in 1896 by the Dowager Marchioness of Londonderry

A 17th century timber-framed forge at Claverdon, WARWICKSHIRE, where the horse-shoe entrance is made of oak

SHEPHERDS

*I be the Shepherd o' the farm: An' be so proud a-roven round,
Wi' my long crook a'thirt my yarm, As if I were a king a-crowned.*

William Barnes, 1801~1886.

Since time immemorial the SHEPHERD cared for
the sheep and oversaw their annual round

Distinctive styles of
smocking and
embroidery developed
for different districts

A "coat smock"
buttoned down the
front, often with horn
buttons.

A "round frock"
slipped over the
head.

Essential dog

The smock developed from a
plain "cover-all" tunic and
it was worn by many farm
workers from the late 1700's
to the late 1800's

Sometimes oiled to keep
out the rain

Length to below the knees
(longer than a farm
labourer's smock).

Leather or canvas gaiters

Oiled boots

HIS WORK

AUGUST to NOVEMBER (according to south or north area). Hiring of Rams and putting them
   to Ewes. Selecting for Market
WINTER. Bringing sheep from the high hills and tending them on lower pastures.

SPRING. Lambing time gave the shepherd long hard days and sleepless nights.
      Salving: i.e. the skin of each sheep was rubbed with tar and rancid
   butter to rid them of infestations. Dipping became compulsory after 1905
MID-MAY to JUNE. Washing sheep in river or pond to clean the wool, followed
   by Shearing, which was usually carried out by a gang of men.

JUNE to JULY. Flocks driven back to the higher hills. Tending and checking them.
AUGUST. Salving or Dipping again in soft soap, soda, arsenic and sulphur.
   Checking for maggot strike, which could quickly kill a sheep in hot weather.

73

Handmade Dorset Buttons, worked in cotton thread over a former, for Smocks, etc.

Bird's Eye

Honeycombe

Singleton
(cloth covered)

Dorset knob

SHEPHERDS on the DOWNS, WOLDS and MARSHES were the farmers' most esteemed employees and were highly valued. A good one was difficult to replace. As a consequence the man was often given a free hand to make decisions on the welfare, breeding and sale of sheep. He had to be a fit man and to enjoy long hours of solitude. Many shepherds learned the job from boyhood, often being taught by their fathers. Over night the sheep were brought to lower ground and the shepherd retired to his farm cottage, but some times, especially at lambing time, he lived in a hut in the hills, amongst his sheep

~DEWPOND~
A dug-out hollow was lined with straw, clay and flints on dry chalk hills. The collected rainwater does not dry out if it is well maintained.

Good Luck Charms

~SHEPHERDS' CROWNS, PURSES or KNEE-CAPS~
Fossils of sea urchins (echinoidea) that occur on on the Downs, in clay-with-flints ground.
(about 1 or 2 inches across)

A "dormer" LANTERN with t-shaped holes in dormers on the crown

A "plain" LANTERN with the metal crown pierced with holes to allow ventilation for the candle

Until about 1915 the lantern windows were made of panels of thin horn.

SOUTHDOWN

Southdowns give extremely fine wool

DORSET HORN

The only English breed which will breed out of season. It produces very fine wool.

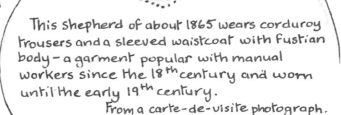

This shepherd of about 1865 wears corduroy trousers and a sleeved waistcoat with fustian body – a garment popular with manual workers since the 18th century and worn until the early 19th century.

From a carte-de-visite photograph.

Until the 18th century sheep had been bred mainly for their WOOL but with the coming of the Industrial Revolution in the 19th century MEAT became important. Experiments in crossing different breeds began to produce both fine wool and good meat.

CROOKS

to catch a sheep by the leg
or, with a wider mouth, a lamb by the neck

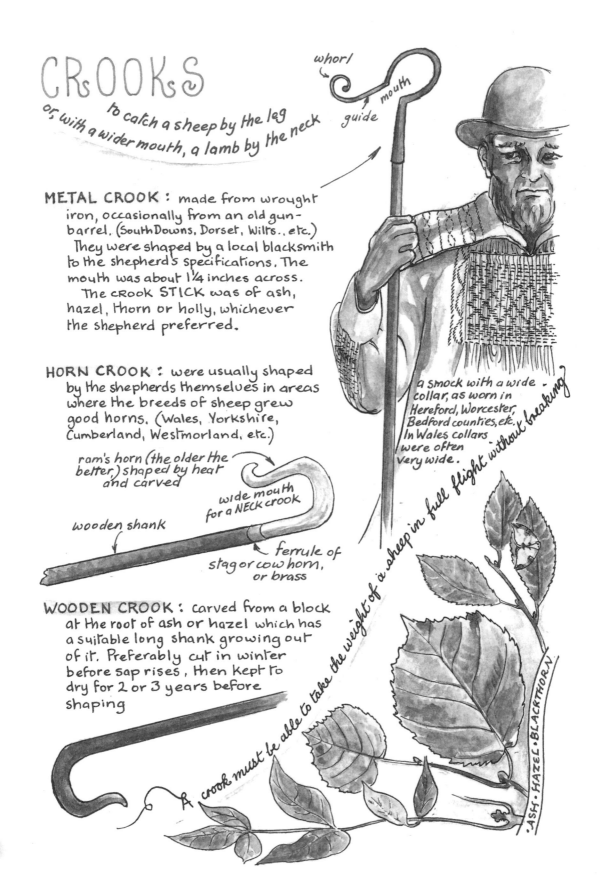

whorl

guide

mouth

METAL CROOK: made from wrought
iron, occasionally from an old gun-
barrel. (South Downs, Dorset, Wilts., etc.)
 They were shaped by a local blacksmith
to the shepherd's specifications. The
mouth was about 1¼ inches across.
 The CROOK STICK was of ash,
hazel, thorn or holly, whichever
the shepherd preferred.

HORN CROOK: were usually shaped
by the shepherds themselves in areas
where the breeds of sheep grew
good horns. (Wales, Yorkshire,
Cumberland, Westmorland, etc.)

ram's horn (the older the
better,) shaped by heat
and carved

wide mouth
for a NECK crook

wooden shank

ferrule of
stag or cow horn,
or brass

a smock with a wide
collar, as worn in
Hereford, Worcester,
Bedford counties, etc.
In Wales collars
were often
very wide.

WOODEN CROOK: carved from a block
at the root of ash or hazel which has
a suitable long shank growing out
of it. Preferably cut in winter
before sap rises, then kept to
dry for 2 or 3 years before
shaping

A crook must be able to take the weight of a sheep in full flight without breaking

•ASH •HAZEL •BLACKTHORN

76

🎵 BELLS 🎵

SWEET MUSIC OF THE HILLS

The Downland shepherds acquired their own bells, which were often passed on from one shepherd to another. They carved the YOKES and LOCKYERS themselves.

Each bell had its own individual tone. The shepherd could tell from the sound of the bells in which direction the sheep were travelling (useful in fog), or if they were agitated.

STRAP COLLAR made of an old cut-up boot.

wide mouth **CANNISTER** from mild steel sheet over-laid with brass, to give a sonorous ring.

A cast brass **BELL**

wood or bone **LOCKYERS**

leather strap

wooden **YOKE** or **CROOK** (sometimes painted)

narrow mouth **CLUCKET** or **CLUNKER**

ting ping ting a ling

tang ring a peeng tang ta-e-ng ping tong

toong tong tong tbong

from
THE SUSSEX AGRICULTURAL EXPRESS 4 NOVEMBER 1848

SHEEP STEALING IN SURREY

We are sorry to hear that the crime of sheep stealing is alarmingly on the increase in the County of Surrey. Within the last ten days or a fortnight no less than fifteen valuable sheep have been stolen from different flocks in the parishes of Leatherhead, Cobham, Walton, etc. So daring have the the thieves become that they kill and skin the animals in or near the folds and within a short distance of the proprietors' dwellings.

77

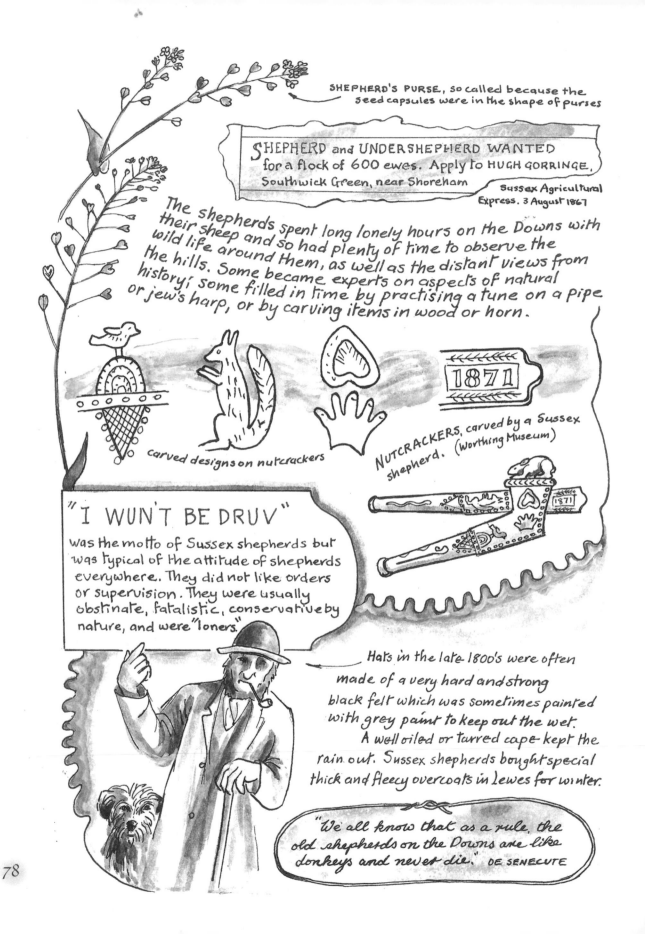

SHEPHERD'S PURSE, so called because the seed capsules were in the shape of purses

SHEPHERD and UNDERSHEPHERD WANTED for a flock of 600 ewes. Apply to HUGH GORRINGE. Southwick Green, near Shoreham

Sussex Agricultural Express. 3 August 1867

The shepherds spent long lonely hours on the Downs with their sheep and so had plenty of time to observe the wild life around them, as well as the distant views from the hills. Some became experts on aspects of natural history; some filled in time by practising a tune on a pipe or jew's harp, or by carving items in wood or horn.

carved designs on nutcrackers

NUTCRACKERS, carved by a Sussex shepherd. (Worthing Museum)

"I WUN'T BE DRUV"

was the motto of Sussex shepherds but was typical of the attitude of shepherds everywhere. They did not like orders or supervision. They were usually obstinate, fatalistic, conservative by nature, and were "loners."

Hats in the late 1800's were often made of a very hard and strong black felt which was sometimes painted with grey paint to keep out the wet.

A well oiled or tarred cape kept the rain out. Sussex shepherds bought special thick and fleecy overcoats in Lewes for winter.

"We all know that as a rule, the old shepherds on the Downs are like donkeys and never die." DE SENECUTE

78

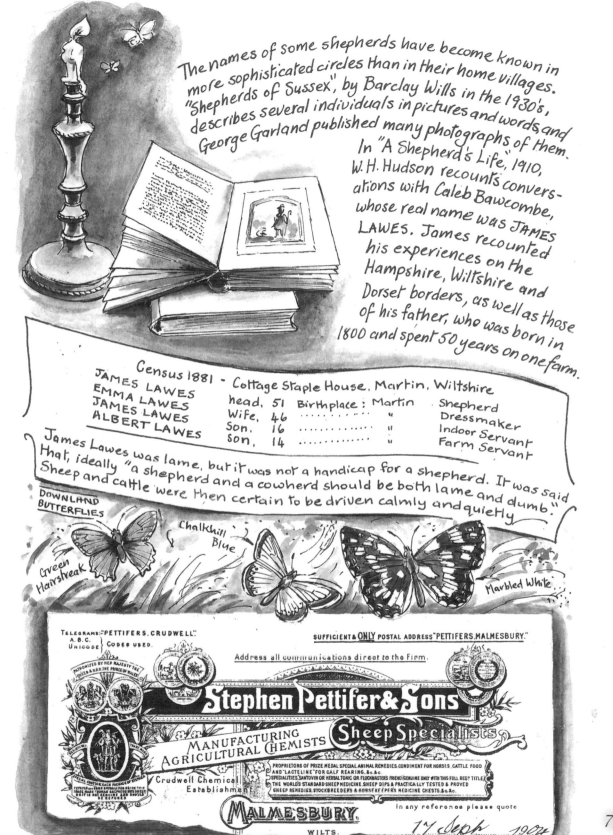

The names of some shepherds have become known in more sophisticated circles than in their home villages. "Shepherds of Sussex", by Barclay Wills in the 1930's, describes several individuals in pictures and words, and George Garland published many photographs of them.

In "A Shepherd's Life," 1910, W.H. Hudson recounts conversations with Caleb Bawcombe, whose real name was JAMES LAWES. James recounted his experiences on the Hampshire, Wiltshire and Dorset borders, as well as those of his father, who was born in 1800 and spent 50 years on one farm.

Census 1881 - Cottage Staple House, Martin, Wiltshire

JAMES LAWES	head, 51	Birthplace: Martin	Shepherd
EMMA LAWES	Wife, 46	"	Dressmaker
JAMES LAWES	Son, 16	"	Indoor Servant
ALBERT LAWES	Son, 14	"	Farm Servant

James Lawes was lame, but it was not a handicap for a shepherd. It was said that, ideally "a shepherd and a cowherd should be both lame and dumb." Sheep and cattle were then certain to be driven calmly and quietly.

DOWNLAND BUTTERFLIES

Green Hairstreak

Chalkhill Blue

Marbled White

TELEGRAMS: "PETTIFERS, CRUDWELL".
A.B.C.
UNICODE } CODES USED.

SUFFICIENT & ONLY POSTAL ADDRESS "PETTIFERS, MALMESBURY."

Address all communications direct to the Firm.

PATRONIZED BY HER MAJESTY THE
QUEEN & H.R.H. THE PRINCE OF WALES

Stephen Pettifer & Sons

MANUFACTURING AGRICULTURAL CHEMISTS

Sheep Specialists

Crudwell Chemical Establishment

PROPRIETORS OF PRIZE MEDAL SPECIAL ANIMAL REMEDIES. CONDIMENT FOR HORSES, CATTLE FOOD AND "LACTELINE" FOR CALF REARING, &c.&c.
SPECIALITIES, SANTOVIN OR HERBAL TONIC OR FLOCKMASTERS' FRIEND (GENUINE ONLY WITH THIS FULL REG? TITLE).
THE WORLD'S STANDARD SHEEP MEDICINE. SHEEP DIPS & PRACTICALLY TESTED & PROVED
SHEEP REMEDIES, STOCKBREEDERS & HORSEKEEPERS MEDICINE CHESTS. &c.&c.

MALMESBURY,
WILTS.

In any reference please quote

17 Sept 1904

79

Lullaby of a Shepherd's Wife.

Anon.

Sleep, baby, sleep,
Thy father watches the sheep,
Thy mother is shaking the
dreamland tree
And down falls a little dream
on thee.
Sleep, baby, sleep.

Sleep, baby, sleep,
The large stars are the sheep,
The little stars are the lambs
I guess,
The fair moon is the shepherdess.
Sleep, baby, sleep.

Yan (1)
Tyan (2)
Tethera (3)
Methera (4)
Pimp (5)
Sethera (6)
Pethera (7)
Hovera (8)
Dovera (9)
Dik (10)

Shepherd's Counting

"I don't say that I want to have my life again, because t'would be sinful. We must take what is sent. But if t'was offered to me and I was told to choose my work, I'd say Give me the Wiltshire Downs again and let me be a shepherd there all my life long."
Caleb Bawcombe (James Lawes)
in A Shepherd's Life.

Evening grey and morning red
Sends the shepherd wet to bed,
Evening red and morning grey,
It's the sign of a very fair day

80

At **LAMBING TIME** shepherds of Downs, Wolds and Marshes spent about 6 weeks alone and isolated, living in a hut amongst their sheep, ready to tend the ewes and lambs, day and night.

Traditional wooden hut

In Kent called "lookers" hut or sheep house

Shafts were attached and the hut was towed onto the hills by a horse. It was equipped with bed, stove, etc. and necessary tools

In later years corrugated iron huts were made.

On the Romney Marshes they were often brick-built and permanent

from a photograph (Dorking Museum)

DAN MARRINER
employed by Mr James of
Box Hill Farm, Dorking, Surrey.
about 1912

Dan wears a "slop", a canvas jacket that covered a multitude of other clothes.

Dan was a Salvationist, a follower of the London Salvation Army, which shocked people in the 1880's, as Salvationists believed in equality of the sexes, they appeared to be militant, disregarded social norms and held street parades and prayer meetings.

81

THE SHEPHERD COULD NOT WORK WITHOUT A SHEEPDOG

Some were Welsh collies: tan and white or blue with patches of black and white

Some were shaggy and bearded collies, others crosses between collie and Old English bobtails

"If he be but with his master, he lies content, indifferent to every surrounding object, seemingly half asleep and half awake, rarely mingling with his kind, rarely courting and generally shrinking from the notice of a stranger: but the moment duty calls, his sleepy listless eye becomes brightened: he eagerly gazes at his master, inquires and comprehends all that he has to do, and, springing up, gives himself to the discharge of his duty with a sagacity and fidelity and devotion, too rarely equalled even by man himself"

William Youatt 1895

Some were black and white Border collies, others cross-breeds

IN BRITAIN THEY WERE TRAINED TO HERD SHEEP RATHER THAN TO GUARD THEM

A "looker" was a dog that would drive sheep along a lane and put its forefeet on a sheep's back so that it could check its master was still in front.

A "road dog" was specially trained to drive animals long distances on roads. It could divide a flock if a vehicle came along and patrol the divided flock.

DOG LICENCES 1867–1988

EXEMPTIONS:
under 6 months old, and hounds under 1 year owned by a Master of Foxhounds
A shepherd was allowed 2 dogs
A farmer was allowed 2 dogs
A farm with over
400 sheep — 3 dogs
1,000 sheep — 4 dogs
for every 500 sheep over 1,000 — 1 extra dog, up to a total of 8 dogs unlicenced

The dogs were tough characters, and, like their masters, endured hard lives.
The shepherd had to provide his dog's food. Many dogs were clever poachers, although not supposed to hunt.

Popular names: Tramp, Sweep, Mot, Fly, Jack, Rex, Watch, Tess, - - - -

82

Folding the Flock

The sheep were kept together by portable HURDLES. Setting them up was heavy work. They were indispensable at lambing time and kept one group of sheep separate from another. They confined them in autumn to fatten them on crops of turnips, swedes or clover. The droppings of these sheep fertilised the ground for a crop the following year.

In rocky and mountainous areas permanent stone walls confined the flock.

"The foot of the sheep turns sand into gold, And riches unmeasured drop on the sheep fold."

Old Saying.

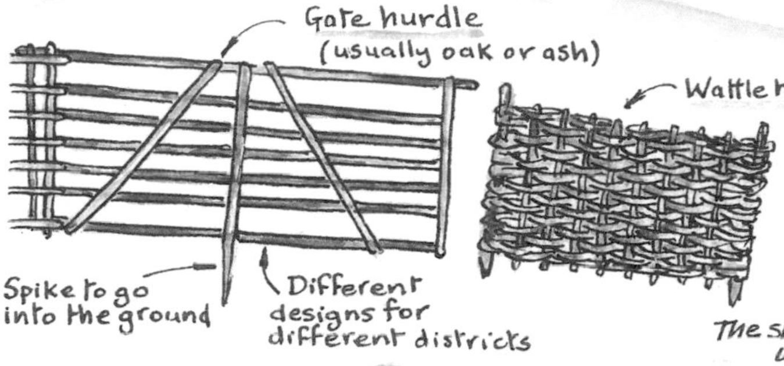

1914
Wearing a traditional shepherd's blanket as a scarf.

Gate hurdle (usually oak or ash)

Wattle hurdle (usually hazel)

Hurdles could be "thatched" with gorse or bracken to give animals protection from bad weather

Spike to go into the ground

Different designs for different districts

The standard size for a FOLD for 100 SHEEP was one chain square. i.e. 22 yards by 22 yards

It is summer, and this shepherd wears a very short smock as he folds his sheep within wattle hurdles. About 1914

SHEARING
late May–June

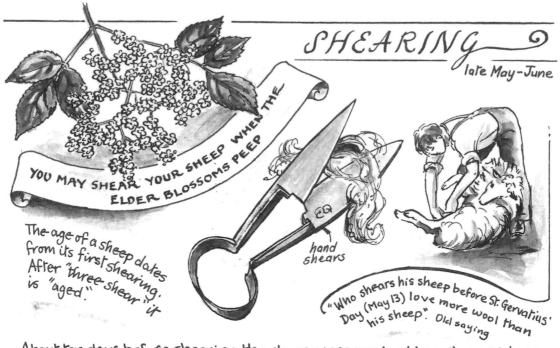

YOU MAY SHEAR YOUR SHEEP WHEN THE ELDER BLOSSOMS PEEP

The age of a sheep dates from its first shearing. After "three shear" it is "aged".

hand shears

"Who shears his sheep before St. Gervatius' Day (May 13) love more wool than his sheep". Old saying

About ten days before shearing the sheep were washed in a river or deep pool. Men stood waist deep in the cold water all day dunking sheep, one after the other, to clean their fleeces. After 1919 washing the animals was not economical and they were usually sheared "in the grease."

For the actual shearing, a gang of travelling shearing men arrived at the farm.

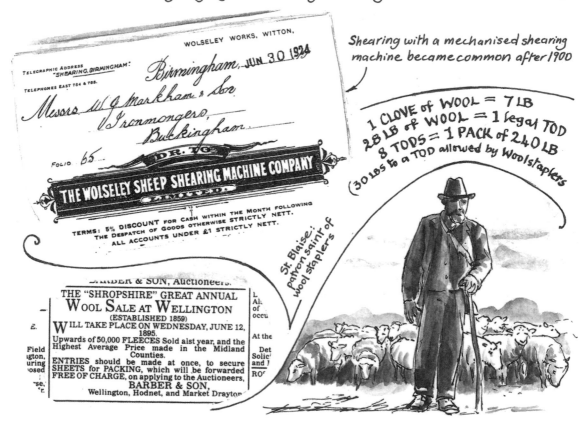

Shearing with a mechanised shearing machine became common after 1900

1 CLOVE of WOOL = 7 LB
28 LB of WOOL = 1 legal TOD
8 TODS = 1 PACK of 240 LB
(30 LBS to a TOD allowed by Woolstaplers

WOLSELEY WORKS, WITTON,
Birmingham, JUN 30 1924
Telegraphic Address "SHEARING, BIRMINGHAM"
Telephones East 754 & 755
Messrs W.G. Markham & Son, Ironmongers, Buckingham
Folio 65
Dr. To
THE WOLSELEY SHEEP SHEARING MACHINE COMPANY
LIMITED
TERMS: 5% DISCOUNT FOR CASH WITHIN THE MONTH FOLLOWING THE DESPATCH OF GOODS OTHERWISE STRICTLY NETT. ALL ACCOUNTS UNDER £1 STRICTLY NETT.

St. Blaise: patron saint of wool staplers

BARBER & SON, Auctioneers.
THE "SHROPSHIRE" GREAT ANNUAL WOOL SALE AT WELLINGTON
(ESTABLISHED 1859)
WILL TAKE PLACE ON WEDNESDAY, JUNE 12, 1895.
Upwards of 50,000 FLEECES Sold last year, and the Highest Average Price made in the Midland Counties.
ENTRIES should be made at once, to secure SHEETS for PACKING, which will be forwarded FREE OF CHARGE, on applying to the Auctioneers, BARBER & SON, Wellington, Hodnet, and Market Drayton

84

TO THE 🐑 FAIR

Agricultural and domestic workers went to the Fairs to seek work, meet friends and neighbours and to have a good time. Shepherds were no exception. The Fair provided one of very few holidays they had.

After delivering their sheep to the sale pens the shepherds were free to join other workers in the public house, where, usually they thoroughly indulged themselves in beer and pies.

At home a shepherd ate such things as boiled pork, fat bacon, cheese, boiled potatoes and cabbage that had been well doused in vinegar. Afterwards a suet pudding would go down well, with some weak tea or beer.

"When I goes dead, as it may hap
Why bury me under the good ale tap!
Wi' voulded arms there let me lie,
Cheek by jowl, my dog and I"
an old rhyme

ESPECIALLY LARGE SHEEP FAIRS

- Warminster, Wilts, about 11th Aug.
- Barnet, London, 5th September
- Findon, West Sussex., early Sept.
- Woodbury Hill, Dorset, 18th Sept.
- Masham, Yorkshire, about 26 Sept. (750,000 sheep)
- Corby Glen, Grantham, Lincs. 4th Oct.
- Weyhill, Hampshire, 10th October
- Yarm Cheese Fair, Cleveland, 20·20 Oct. (500 tons of cheese and sheep on the third day)
- Gig Fair, Newhaven, Derbys. 30th Oct.

~BEER~

"Stingo" – very strong.
"Huff Cap" ~ a brew that soon set a man's hat at a rakish angle.
"Black Strap" ~ a dark-coloured brew.
"Old October" ~ strong and usually kept for after Christmas

A Shepherd's Toast

"If I had store,
By sheep and fold
I'd give you gold
But, since I'm poor,
By crook and bell
I wish you well."

The day arrives of the autumn fair
  And torrents fall.
Though sheep in throngs are gathered there
  Ten thousand all
Sodden, with hurdles round them reared;
And lot by lot the pens are cleared.
	The auctioneer wrings out his beard,
	And wipes his book bedrenched and smeared
	And rakes the rain from his face with
	       the edge of his hand,
	  As torrents fall.
	Thomas Hardy. 1840-1928

The decline of Shepherds on the Downs

Australian wool began to flood the markets in the early 1900's and the price of wool fell. The land previously grazed by sheep was ploughed and so shepherds who had watched the flocks for centuries on Downs, Wolds and Marshes were no longer needed.

By the 1930's there were few Downland shepherds working. Some of them had spent all their working days on one farm. They lived long lives, but as they had spent so much time out in bad weather, they suffered from rheumatism and bronchitis

After the turn of the century good thick woollen cloth was not so easily available. The shepherd often wore a second-hand cavalry or army great-coat, if he could obtain one.

Old Shepherd's Prayer

Heavenly Master, I would like to wake to they same green places where I be knowed for breaking dogs and follerin' sheep.
And if I may not walk in the old ways and look in th' old faces, I would sooner sleep

Charlotte Mew 1870~1928 ~

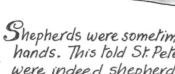

Shepherds were sometimes buried with tufts of wool in their hands. This told St. Peter at the gates of heaven that they were indeed shepherds and so their occupation had prevented them from attending church every Sunday,

Shepherds of Mountain and Moorland

Shepherds of these regions still follow today a similar way of life to that of their predecessors down the ages.

In rugged terrain the sheep roam freely, but are checked regularly by a shepherd who must be exceptionally fit. On easier slopes he often rode on horseback. His dogs retrieved sheep from craggy peaks that were unreachable for humans. Sheep were brought down to lower pastures for lambing, shearing, sorting, etc., where permanent stone walls confined them, instead of the portable hurdles that were used by Lowland and Downland shepherds.

Tom Shimwell of Long Roods Farm, nr. Bakewell, Derbyshire. 1928

Tom still wears short trousers although he was 15 years old in 1928. He was one of eight children, five of them boys who all went into farming. Tom married and farmed Red House Farm nearby, whilst two of his brothers stayed on at Long Roods. They won many prizes at shows for their sheep.

Carrying a weak Herdwick back for attention at the farm. Cumberland.

EAR MARKING

Each mark is distinctive for a particular farm

Sheep in rocky hills and mountains could not be closely watched. They established grazing areas, (heaths) that were passed down, ewe to lamb, over generations, but some did stray away onto another farmer's land.

TO MAKE IT EASIER FOR THE SHEPHERD TO IDENTIFY HIS SHEEP A SYSTEM OF MARKS, NICKED BY SHEARS, IN THE SHEEPS' EARS, MADE (and still make) THEM RECOGNISABLE.

The shepherd could recognise his own sheep anywhere from the marks

Both ears are cut "Sciw" for TAN-Y-FOEL, Llanfachreth, Merioneth, North Wales

The mark represents the farm and not the family living there.

It is not known when ear marks began. In Wales a register of marks for an area near Dolgellau dates from about 1825. The first guide for the Eastern Fells of Cumberland was compiled by Joseph Walker of Martindale in 1817.

Thomas Wilson (of Keswick) catalogued about 1,600 identification marks for Cumberland, Westmorland, and Furness. Wilson's "Shepherd's Guide" was published in 1908

Upper fold bitted rear ear

Forked near ear Coloured "smit" marks on the wool were also for identification

The ear mark of HAUSE FARM, Martindale, Cumberland.

MARKING IRONS

In order to identify sheep if they
strayed they were, in the 1800's, skin branded
with a hot iron. Later, the iron was dipped into
hot pitch instead, and sheep were marked after each shearing, but
the pitch could spoil the wool for marketing. Instead, a red dye, "rudd",
could be used which would wash out in the woollen mills.

HERDWICK Ram, Cumbria

WELSH MOUNTAIN Ewe

SWALEDALE Ewe-
Northern Counties

Rose and Charles Farrow of
Hutton le Hole, Yorkshire, in the 1930's

THE BELL WETHER: In mountainous
country, such as Cumberland, an old
wether (castrated ram) sometimes wore a bell, which not
only helped the shepherd
locate the flock, but
aided in holding the
sheep together on
their home
"heath".

In England and Wales

1921: Shepherds:	11,240	1931: Shepherds: 10,298
Shepherdesses:	42	Shepherdesses: 25

DAIRYMAIDS and COWMEN

Victorian Scrap

"I rise up in the early morn
my labour to pursue,
And with my yoke and milking pails
I trudge the morning dew
My cows to milk, and there I taste the
sweets which nature yields;
The lark doth sing to welcome me
into the flowery fields"
Folk Song

In 1845 there were very few large herds of cattle. Farmers and small-holders kept a few cows for their own and their neighbours' milk. As the century progressed and the railway system developed, milk could be transported for sale and herds of both beef and dairy cattle grew larger.

Farmers who kept a herd of dairy cows too large for them to manage themselves employed a COWMAN If the herd did not take up all of his time he would be engaged upon general farm work.

_____ With a small number of cows the farmer's wife often acted as DAIRYMAID but when there were many of them a hired woman, or several of them, were employed to help with milking and the making of butter and cheese.

90

The never-ending task for cowmen and dairy maids was MILKING~ in the mornings and evenings, every day of the week.

One milker could milk a dozen cows in about 90 minutes. Five milkers were required for 60 cows.

In WINTER the cows came into the cow-shed, or shippon, to be milked. In SUMMER they were, until the early 1900's, often milked in the fields.

Dairy maids, about 1900

As late as 1942, on the SOMERSET LEVELS, C. Henry Warren reported that hundreds of cows, mostly Friesians, grazed in flowery meadows beside the rhines (dykes). He saw milking stools lying beside a hedge and a bundle of horse-hair "spans" for hobbling the cows at milking time. The milkers came, morning and evening, bowling along the lanes in their horse-drawn milk floats. They drove the cows into a corner of the meadow and milked them there.

Skull caps were often worn by milkers, as they had to press their foreheads into the cow's flank. A hat brim would protrude too much.

MILKING TIME.

"A pint of milk for Elsie please, Let it be cool and sweet. She wants to drink it quickly now, It's not for washing her feet."

Postcard sent in 1908 to Miss Elsie Kidd, The Mill House, Kings Langley, Herts., from "Daddy", who wrote the verse.

91

"A DAIRY WOMAN'S HANDS SHOULD BE SMOOTH AS *Butter*, WHITE AS *Milk* AND COOL AS *Spring Water*." (Kept soft with goose fat and lard)

A cow is always hand milked on her right side

"A CROSS COW HOLDS UP HER MILK" Emerson 1870

A comfortable cow with a quick experienced milker will produce more milk, which is richer in butter-fat, than with a slow, clumsy milker.

IN THE DAIRY

Most farms had the dairy on the north side of the house where it was cool, for milk soured and butter would not "come" in warm conditions. There was a scrubbed stone or brick floor, marble slabs and well scoured tables and utensils.

china milk pail

PURE MILK

metal cream skimmer (fleeter)

wooden butter runner

hand carved wooden butter stamp

WEST HA... WARLINGH...

PURE DEVONSHIRE CLOTTED CREAM

metal milk can

china pot

waxed card cream pots

Pure Rich Cream

"You can't do better than to put plenty of water into the milk provided you first put it through the cow." B.A. Steward

A COW NEEDS FROM 6 TO 20 GALLONS OF WATER A DAY ACCORDING TO HER MILK YIELD AND THE SEASON —

MILKING TIME.

R. Braid.

92

The first milk after the calf is born is extra rich and salty and it continues for four days. It is called BIESTINGS or BEESTINGS and contains essential nutrients for the new-born calf. A small amount was often milked off for making a pie, which was considered a delicacy by some, but was disliked by others. The pie was made by baking the beestings in a slow oven with sugar and topping it with grated nutmeg.

Phil Drabble, country writer, was invited for lunch at a farm. The baked 'custard', which was served with stewed fruit, tasted very strange to him, 'like rancid cheese'. He discovered afterwards that it had been made from beestings.

Perennial Rye Grass

Meadow Fescue

Cocksfoot

Meadow Foxtail

Crested Dogstail

Tall Oat Grass

They strolled down the lane together
The sky was studded with stars ~
They reached the gate in silence ~
And he lifted down the bars ~
She neither smiled nor thanked him
Because she knew not how;
For he was just a farmer's boy
And she was a Jersey cow! *Anon.*

Grasses enjoyed by Cattle

Some plants, such as mint, water parsnip, wild garlic, ox-eye daisy, hawkweed, yarrow, tansy, can affect cows and their milk. Turnips flavour the milk if eaten shortly before milking.

93

14, FRIARGATE,

WORKS,—BAMBER'S YARD,

Preston, _Mar_ 1882

Messrs P. Howarth & Co

BOUGHT OF BAMBER & CO.,

CHURN MAKERS, &c.

August 26th 1891

To Messrs Adam & Son

Oakham.

Memorandum from

THE YORKSHIRE WOLDS CREAMERY

TRADE MARK.

HUNMANBY.

Edw Keighley

TELEPHONE Nos

HEAD OFFICE ...... 14 SLOUGH
BAYLIS COURT FARM ... 35
WINDSOR .... 24 WINDSOR
MANOR FARM 43
(OLD WINDSOR)

TELEGRAPHIC ADDRESS PURSER SLOUGH

MANOR FARM,

OLD WINDSOR. 190

BOUGHT OF

E. V. A. Purser

DAIRY FARMERS.

MANOR FARM.

OLD WINDSOR.

Baylis Court Farm. SLOUGH

Grove Farm. LANGLEY

SPECIAL ALDERNEY & JERSEY COWS KEPT FOR INFANTS & INVALIDS

The "Monarch" Milk Carrier.

THE MONARCH MILK CARRIER

W. LAWRENCE
FROM COW
TO BOTTLE
PHOENIX COURT DAIRY

Cardboard Top for reusable glass bottle

A Short-horn bull about 1905

The Champion.

94

STOCKMAN

was a term that came into use in this country in the 1880's to describe a man employed especially to deal with livestock, usually large herds of either beef or dairy cattle.

His work included milking, rearing calves, fattening cattle, care of the bull, breeding and showing, etc. He decided on the best diet for the animals in his care. Grass and hay was supplemented by brewers' grains and linseed jelly mixed with chaff. After 1918 oil cakes with balanced ingredients were commercially made. They contained cotton-seed, linseed, ground nut, copra, palm kernel, rape seed, soya bean, etc. Cattle were also fed on bran, malt culms, maize, sugar beet, molasses and fish meal. Roots such as mangolds were given in winter.

TO THRIVE:
Cattle should be kept to a routine and not be hurried, struck, or shouted at.

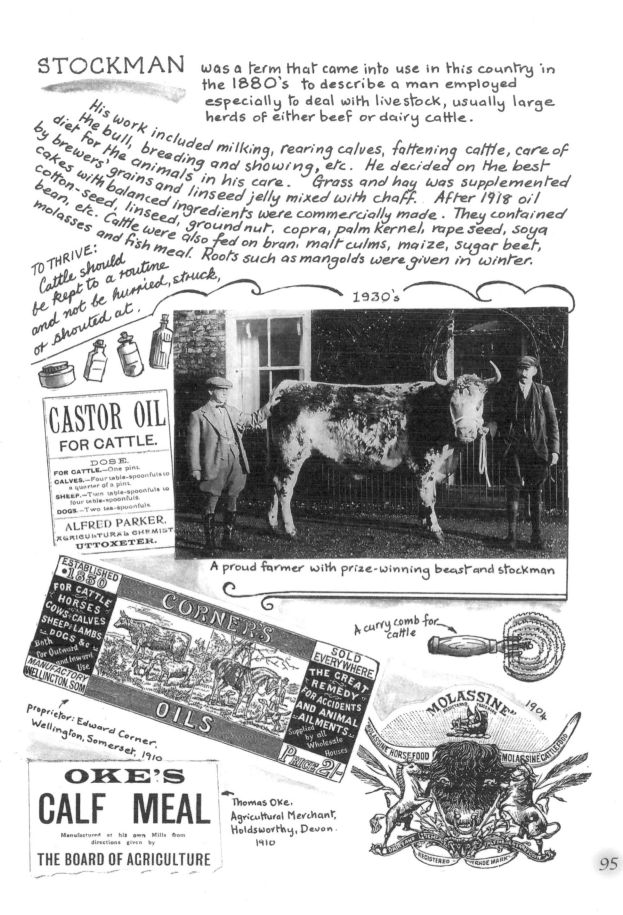

1930's

A proud farmer with prize-winning beast and stockman

CASTOR OIL
FOR CATTLE.

DOSE.
FOR CATTLE.—One pint.
CALVES.—Four table-spoonfuls to a quarter of a pint.
SHEEP.—Two table-spoonfuls to four table-spoonfuls.
DOGS.—Two tea-spoonfuls.

ALFRED PARKER,
AGRICULTURAL CHEMIST,
UTTOXETER.

ESTABLISHED 1850
FOR CATTLE
HORSES
COWS CALVES
SHEEP LAMBS
DOGS &c
Both for Outward and Inward Use
MANUFACTORY
WELLINGTON. SOM.

CORNER'S OILS

SOLD EVERYWHERE
THE GREAT REMEDY FOR ACCIDENTS AND ANIMAL AILMENTS
Supplied by all Wholesale Houses
PRICE 2/-

Proprietor: Edward Corner, Wellington, Somerset, 1910

A curry comb for cattle

MOLASSINE 1904
MOLASSINE HORSE FOOD   MOLASSINE CATTLE FOOD

OKE'S
CALF MEAL
Manufactured at his own Mills from directions given by
THE BOARD OF AGRICULTURE

Thomas Oke.
Agricultural Merchant,
Holdsworthy, Devon.
1910

95

The BULL is HALF the HERD
(old saying)

BEEF BREEDS:-
Hereford, Shorthorn, North Devon, Sussex, Welsh, Aberdeen Angus, Galloway, Highland.

The Midland Counties become famous for fat cattle, as the type of soil there produced good grass on which they thrived.

Sirloin Steak →

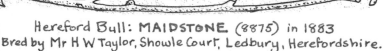

Hereford Bull: MAIDSTONE (8875) in 1883
Bred by Mr H W Taylor, Showle Court, Ledbury, Herefordshire.

Cattle breeders were usually well-to-do farmers with many acres. They often chose elaborate names for their bulls, who were entered in the pedigree Herd Books. The pedigree cows usually had simple names, such as DAISY, CHERRY or BEAUTY. However MAIDSTONE'S great granddam was DUCHESS, a daughter of PRINCE ALBERT and VICTORIA

A Hereford bull, SERVILIUS, (9201) who was bred by Mr. S Robinson of Kington, Hereford, and exported to the USA, had a run of female ancestors with the pretty names of RED ROSE, WILD ROSE, MOSS ROSE and ROSE of WARWICK.

A Hereford bull and owner, with some well thatched ricks in the background. About 1895 (from a photograph)

96

In 1933 MILK MARKETING BOARDS were set up and in 1936 County Council Authorities became responsible for testing milk for tuberculosis. A herd that was licenced and attested had to be kept apart and fenced away from other cattle and from poultry.

FARMERS WITH ATTESTED HERDS RECEIVED A HIGHER PRICE FOR THE MILK

"When the cows came in, each one entering her customary stall and pulling at the hay that awaited her in the rack, Dad tethered each one by her chain. The cow shed grew warm and the smell of the cows was sweet and comforting. Dad switched his cap front to back, so that the peak wouldn't jam into the cow's flank, picked up the pail and sat down to milk. The milk sang into the pail in an uninterrupted stream. Occasionally, if we children were hovering near and Dad was feeling skittish, he would direct a squirt of milk into our faces and laugh when we squealed." Author.

MILKING BREEDS: Shorthorn, Jersey Guernsey, South Devon, Ayrshire British Holstein, Red Poll, Kerry Lincoln Red, Friesian, Dexter

Milking machines became more popular for large herds in the 1930's but older farm hands thought the cows weren't comfortable with them and they gave less milk.

24 May 1938. Farmer & Stockbreeder Cowman, married, for new accredited herd; experienced milkers only need apply. Cottage and good wages. Sessions, Ford Place, Wrotham, Kent

1938 Nearly three-quarters of the agricultural output of the country was from cattle and sheep, fed on grass.

1942

Buy Dairy Cows with a Warranty.
CAMBRIDGE CATTLE MARKET.
GRAIN & CHALK
will Sell by Auction
60 DAIRY-COWS AND HEIFERS, well bred and mostly by Pedigree Bulls and warranted sound.
200 HOME-BRED STORE CATTLE.
EVERY MONDAY at 12 O'CLOCK.
Special Sales of Horses and Agricultural Machinery held periodically.
Auctioneers' Offices: 8, Rose Crescent; and 11, Alexandra Street, Cambridge.

1940's During the War grassland had to be ploughed to produce arable crops. Cattle herds were reduced as there was less grazing land.

Antonio 3rd of Fordmoor

1940's. Showing a Guernsey Bull.

Purchased 1943 by Sir William Rootes, Stype Grange Hungerford, Herts. for 3,400 guineas, a record price for a Guernsey at Public Auction.

DROVERS

And over the highways and byeways I plod,
My clothes are all tattered, my feet are ill shod,
But there isn't a roadway that I haven't trod
Being forty-five summers a drover.

Packie-Manus Byrne

The DROVER bought or collected cattle and sheep from farmers and he drove them in large herds, often for great distances, over a period of two or three weeks, to markets in towns and cities. Before the advent of banks he returned home with the money from the sale of the animals to pay to their former owners. Thus he had to be honest and trustworthy.

A drover had to be licenced, a married man and at least 30 years old, as well as being a householder.

R.S. Surtees, 1845, wrote that drovers wore distinctive and varied clothes: broad-brimmed hats with turn-pike tickets tucked into the bands; some in smock frocks, some in coats of Cambrian "freeze", with fancy buttons decorated with coronets, horses' heads, foxes. Even their gaiters might be fastened with buttons of coloured glass

With the coming of the RAILWAYS the old style of driving animals for long distances gradually came to an end.

In 1848 there were 5000 miles of rail track but railways had not penetrated country-wide so some long distance drives still continued ——➤

~ JOURNEYS BY DROVE ROADS ~

FARMER
bred the animals

↓

DROVER
conducted them to market

↓

SALESMAN
sold at the fair or market

↓

JOBBER
bought them for fattening and resale

↓

CARCASE SALESMAN
Killed them and sold the carcases

↓

BUTCHER
Sold to the general public

The Drover was in complete charge of the animals, up to 1000 or more. He hired helpers and arranged for cattle to be shod, as their hooves would be worn down over the long journey.
Each beast had to have its legs tied and to be thrown on its side by a "feller" or "over-thrower". A smith, working with a boy could shoe about 60-70 beasts a day. Sometimes only the outer side of each hoof would be shod.
Cattle travelling from Anglesey had to swim across the Menai Straits to the Caernarvon shore. In Scotland they swam from the Isle of Skye to the mainland.

Sprigs of Rowan were worn by Welsh drovers to ward off evil on the long arduous journey.

The DROVE ROADS (also called Drift Ways)
were traditional routes from time immemorial, crisscrossing the country. Cattle and sheep travelled on them during spring, summer and autumn from remote parts of England, Ireland, Scotland and Wales

A Drove Road over the lonely Teesdale Moors

GEORGE BORROW, in 1854, encountered MR. BOS, a drover, when travelling in North Wales. He was about forty years old, with a broad red face, pimples, and a wide mouth. "He was dressed in a 'pepper-and-salt' coat of the Newmarket cut, breeches of corduroy and brown top boots, and had on his head a broad, black, coarse, low-crowned hat. In his left hand he held a heavy whale-bone whip with a brass head".

He informed George Borrow that droving was not such a low-life occupation as pig jobbing, that he was known in every public house between Anglesey and Worcester, and that of all the places in England that he had been to he liked Northampton best — not for the ill-tempered men but for the women, who were quite the opposite.

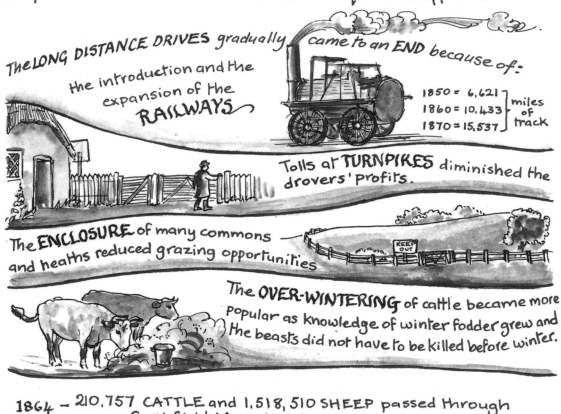

The LONG DISTANCE DRIVES gradually came to an END because of:

the introduction and the expansion of the RAILWAYS

1850 = 6,621 ⎤
1860 = 10,433 ⎬ miles of track
1870 = 15,537 ⎦

Tolls at TURNPIKES diminished the drovers' profits.

The ENCLOSURE of many commons and heaths reduced grazing opportunities

KEEP OUT

The OVER-WINTERING of cattle became more popular as knowledge of winter fodder grew and the beasts did not have to be killed before winter.

1864 — 210,757 CATTLE and 1,518,510 SHEEP passed through Smithfield Market in London

1870 — All cattle from Wales were transported by RAIL

DROVERS were still in demand for driving animals to the railway stations and from the stations to the markets. Many became cattle dealers themselves.

On the droves the cattle had to be kept in good condition in order to make the best prices on arrival at market.

After travelling 12-16 miles a day they stopped overnight to graze on COMMONS or HEATHS or at pre-arranged halts at farms and fields.

The Drover and his senior hirelings spent the nights in farms or inns, or, if there was no accommodation near the grazing, he and his helpers slept rough in barns or sheds or under hedges.

A Shorthorn Cow, about 1850

THE DROVER'S DOG

The **DOG** was the drover's greatest helper. It was usually a cross-breed, a little larger than a shepherd's collie, bred to be courageous and clever, and it was often fierce.

Although valuable and indispensable the dog was treated harshly and had a rough life. Many of its meals were bread and beer.

After the cattle were sold the drover might travel home by coach. It has been reported that sometimes his dog found its own way home by foot, being fed on its journey at inns where it had stopped before. Its food would be paid for by its master on the next drove.

Complete trust could be placed on the dog. A cattle dealer of Alston, Cumberland, wagered that his dog could drive a mixed herd of sheep and oxen nine miles through other grazing herds to Alston market. The dog managed to do this alone, arriving with all the animals in his charge and barking at the door of the person who was usually there to receive them.

Around the turn of the century DROVERS would still drive some animals to market and would stay away from home, in lodgings, two or three nights a week. At the market they would ask those who had just bought animals if the job of driving them to the farm had been taken. With their dogs they drove bullocks and sheep together, the bullocks in front and the sheep behind

THE DROVERS' ARMS, SMITHFIELD, BIRMINGHAM, early 1900's

2 December 1929
From 'Farmer and Stockbreeder':
Shepherd's Dog and Bitch, fetch, drive cattle and sheep any distances, young one offering well. Sowerby, Town Head, Kirkby Stephen.

WATERS & SON'S
ACLE STOCK MART.
Delivered to Mr. _____ 19__
All Accounts not paid on day of sale are payable at
30, CATTLE MARKET, NORWICH
Interest of ¼d. per pound per week charged on accounts outstanding after 14 days.

Lot	Pen	Number	Price per head	£	s.	d.

By 1945 livestock was transported in cattle trucks by road and rail. Drovers continued to help at the markets with loading and unloading, they themselves also doing some buying and selling

Telephone 189
Mr. Rocock
Aug 12
Bot. of C. S. TYRRELL & SON
Family Butchers
11 Western Road,
BEXHILL-ON-SEA
1 Week's Credit Only Allowed
Families Waited Upon Daily
1940

Phones: NOTTINGHAM 43979
Branch: HARBY 229
Member of N.F.U.
14596
KELLAMS
Prop.: W. KELLAM
Horse and Cattle Transport
31 Twells Street
NOTTINGHAM
Mr. Bennd
Radcliffe
May 1945

The occupation of droving disappeared as most drovers gradually moved into cattle dealing

The AGRICULTURAL LABOURER

The labourer carried out almost any rural task that was asked of him: farm work, wood-cutting quarrying, clay-digging, stone breaking and general navvying

His employment relied upon his physical strength. When that failed, through accident, sickness or old age, he received no income at all.
If he was living in a tied cottage it was likely that he could be evicted.

IF YE BE WILLING AND OBEDIENT YE SHALL EAT THE GOOD OF THE LAND *ISIAH 1:19*

BUT IF YE REFUSE AND REBEL. YE SHALL BE DEVOURED WITH THE SWORD: FOR THE MOUTH OF THE LORD HATH SPOKEN IT.

No one passing through the countryside could have been unaware of the labourers working in the fields. They were part of the landscape and their work helped to shape it.

The manual labourer was the lowest in the hierarchy of country workers but he could rise on the social scale by acquiring a special skill, for instance in shepherding or horsemanship.

The Labourer was usually respectful to all above him. He accepted authority and was obedient, even if sometimes resentful. He was generally resigned to his hard life, with its long hours, meagre wages, and living from 'hand to mouth' in a primitive cottage. He was rough and ignorant because he knew no other way. He could be cruel to his family and animals. A soft attitude signified weakness, harshness was the accepted normality

OLD COTTAGE, CANNOCK CHASE, RUGELEY.

COTTAGES were very small, with only one or two rooms, and they were usually overcrowded. Water came from a stream or well and sanitation was non-existent or primitive, however there was often a sty for the pig and a garden. The prospect of going into the workhouse was always present. No work, for any reason, meant no income at all.

JAMES BOWD, of Swavesey, in Cambridgeshire began his married life in 1849. He had a bed, a family bible and three shillings that he had saved. At first the couple lived with his parents. Their little girl was born and his wife had a hard labour. James was as fond of his wife "as a cat with new milk" but he did not tell her how much he loved her because, in his position as head of the house, she might think him weak. They eventually found their own lodgings: two rooms adjoining a blacksmith's shop, with no garden, at £3.10s a year. He thought it a high rent, especially as the blacksmith began hammering at four in the morning and the cobbler on the other side hammered until ten at night.

"Yes, I be always at work, but I be poor for all that. I h'ant but eight shillin' a week – that ben't much to make six-of-family rich, be it? ...... "Do any of your children get employment?"

"Yes, one be at work now. He be twelve years old and gets two shillin' a week, and my wife be gone today to hoe wheat on the farm over that side...... and we ha' had a loaf of bread from the parish for one young 'un, but I ben't sure as we shall get the loaf now when so many of us be at work..... It ben't easy out of our income to get a belly-ful for so many, be it?"

— a labourer encountered by Alexander Somerville

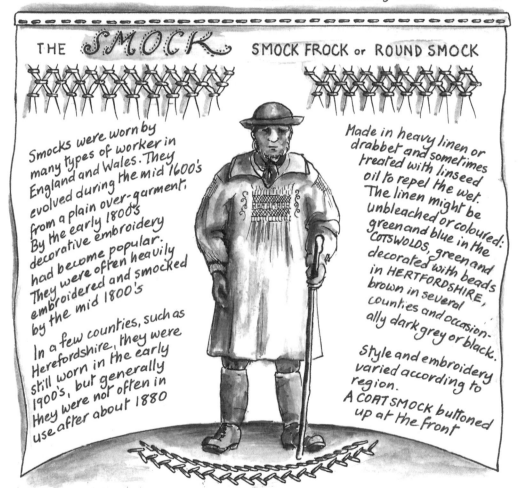

THE SMOCK   SMOCK FROCK or ROUND SMOCK

Smocks were worn by many types of worker in England and Wales. They evolved during the mid 1600's from a plain over-garment. By the early 1800's decorative embroidery had become popular. They were often heavily embroidered and smocked by the mid 1800's

In a few counties, such as Herefordshire, they were still worn in the early 1900's, but generally they were not often in use after about 1880

Made in heavy linen or drabbet and sometimes treated with linseed oil to repel the wet. The linen might be unbleached or coloured: green and blue in the COTSWOLDS, green and decorated with beads in HERTFORDSHIRE, brown in several counties and occasionally dark grey or black.

Style and embroidery varied according to region.

A COAT SMOCK buttoned up at the front

LENHAM AGRICULTURAL ASSOCIATION   (near Maidstone, Kent)
~ PRIZES AWARDED ~ 27 October 1848 ~

Length of Servitude: £2 to DANIEL HOPE. 42 years servitude with Mr. F. B. Elvy

Yearly Servitude: £2 to JOHN WAGHORN. 38 years servitude with Mr. F. B. Elvy

Largest Families without Parochial Relief: £2 to JOHN CLACKETT servant of Mr. James Hatch, for having maintained 8 children under 14 years of age.

Sussex Agric. Express 4 November 1848

CANON GIRDLESTON
of Halburton, Devon

Was very sympathetic to the labourers who were extremely harshly treated by the farmers in Devon. Their wages were very low, their hovels were miserable and poor and many households were starving.

Between **1866-1872** the Canon organised a migration of **4-5000** labouring families that lived in Devon, to various other counties where the pay and the housing were better.

The Canon became very unpopular in his area. He was ostracised by farmers, gentry and fellow clergymen, but by 1880 conditions in his parish were improved.

from a carte-de-visite

Photographed in the late 1860's or early 70's by "Mr A. Simmonds from London", who would have travelled into the country and set up a temporary studio in a village.

The sitter wears a fairly new tweed coat with wide lapels, over a long cloth waistcoat. He sports a bright check scarf and his trousers appear to be of 'moleskin'.

HARVEST HORN
about 18 inches long, made of tin.
It was blown at harvest time, particularly in East Anglia, by the "Lord," or leader of the harvest, to summon the workers at 5 a.m., and to herald meal times.

The Flail was called "Stick and a Half" in Suffolk, "Poverty Stick" in Cambridgeshire.

Handle often made of ash

Hinge of iron, leather, eel skin or green ash

Swingel of hardwood, such as holly, blackthorn or crab apple

FLAIL
4 to 5 feet long, made of hardwood
To thresh out the grain the straw was beaten with the swingel on a barn floor. Doors on either side of the building created a draught which blew the chaff from the heavier grain. The work was hard, skilful and monotonous.

Three Cheers for Arch and the Union

Back in the 1830's desperate conditions for farm labourers brought about a revolt in Tolpuddle, Dorset. Farmers refused to increase the mens' pitifully low wages. As a result of taking an unlawful oath six "TOLPUDDLE MARTYRS" were transported to Australia. Despite further protests and riots very little progress was made in improving the situation of the farm labourers.

IT WAS NOT UNTIL 1872 THAT A LEADER WAS FOUND TO HELP THE LABOURERS TO FORM A NATIONAL UNION

JOSEPH ARCH

was age 46. He had been a crow-scarer as a boy, then a plough-boy, followed by a jobbing labourer, a gravel digger, then wood-cutter. He became an expert mower and hedge-layer, earning enough to buy his own cottage. He was a speaker for the Primitive Methodists.

On WEDNESDAY EVENING, 14th FEBRUARY, 1872 at WELLESBOURNE, WARWICKSHIRE,

a throng of labourers, too many to crowd into The Stag's Head, gathered together after a long day's work, under the village chestnut tree. It was a wet night. Lantern light shone upon their care-worn faces as Joseph Arch stood on a pig-killing stool to speak to them. He spoke for an hour, to those he called "the white slaves of England".

This was the real beginning of:
the NATIONAL AGRICULTURAL LABOURERS UNION
founded in Leamington Spa, 28 May 1872

"All hail Joseph Arch, the labourer's friend,
  The cause he espoused was the weak to defend,
His efforts have been the oppressed to raise,
  Come join hand in hand and sing to his praise." J. Gwyer, 1872

• 1875 • Joseph Arch visited Tolpuddle to make a presentation to one of the old Tolpuddle Martyrs who had returned from Australia. The other five had also returned but they had emigrated to Canada

Harvest Time

The Lord of the Harvest, or Lead, cut the corn slightly ahead of the other workers and set the pace.

SCYTHE - was adaptable and was altered to suit the man using it. An expert old man could work better and swing it more easily than an inexperienced young one.

PITCH FORK was used to toss hay to dry it and to lift hay and sheaves of corn onto the wagon and rick.

This man carries a "flail" basket which holds his lunch, and, over his shoulder a "cradle" attachment for his scythe.

RAKE for gathering dry hay into windrows and collecting up loose corn lying on the stubble.

A CARRYING KERCHIEF made from 1 square yard of cotton cloth. It was carried over the shoulder instead of a 'frail'.

SAND HORN (about 15 ins. long)

A horn, with iron attachments, containing grease and sand for use on a strickle to sharpen the scythe

horn CUP

Wooden COSTREL for beer (about 8 inches long)

"TRAILING BEER" was bought from fines paid to the leader by anyone who trampled on the standing crop.

THE HIRING FAIR

Fairs became fewer in the late 1800's after advertising in newspapers became common

"A SERVANT AND A COCK SHOULD BE KEPT FOR ONE YEAR ONLY"

old saying.

An Agricultural Wages Act of 1919 changed the practice of hiring for a 12-month period

Called GIGLET FAIR (West Country), STATIS or STATTY (Eastern Counties) – from "statute", MOP (Midlands). Sometimes a RUNAWAY FAIR was held one week later.

If work could not be obtained locally or by word of mouth, the only option was to attend a fair and to stand in the town square with all the others who hoped for work. Such fairs were held annually in many towns.

"Can'st plough, thresh, stack, cart muck manage three horses abreast, hedge and ditch? Ar't a single man?"

"Be it a four-horse place sir?"

i.e. an arable farm of about 100 acres.

The acceptance of a FASTENING PENNY or "fest" bound the servant to work for one year, no matter how unpleasant the new situation turned out to be ⟶.

Those seeking employment often wore or carried something to indicate the type of work they sought. e.g. a wisp of wool for a shepherd, whipcord for a carter, etc.

HIRING FAIRS were notorious for drunkenness, fights and riots, as the labourers spent their previous year's wages enjoying themselves before they embarked upon another year of drudgery and servitude.

THE IRISH

In 1841 there were about 400,000 IRISH IMMIGRANTS living in Britain. Then the disastrous famine in Ireland, between 1845-50, when BLIGHT attacked and destroyed the POTATOES on which most of the Irish country people relied, sent hordes of the starving people overseas to find food and work.

Thousands of Irish labourers descended upon the land and they continued to come throughout the century, often travelling from farm to farm doing temporary work and living rough in barns and outhouses. In three months they could earn enough to pay a year's rent on their own farms in Ireland.

CENSUS 1851 March 30/31st	CENSUS 1881 April 3/4th
Stratford Rd. Stratford-upon-Avon, Warws.	Middle Park Farm, Selly Oak, Warws. 118 acres.
The lodging house keeper: MARY McDERMOT was age 64, herself born in Ireland.	The farmer: M.F. RAYBOULD, age 57, had a wife and 8 children (2 sons helped on the farm)
JOHN CONNOR, age 46 ⎫ all agricultural MICHAEL FRAIN, age 29 ⎬ labourers born JOHN SMITH, age 21 ⎪ in Ireland. PATRICK MALONEY, age 20 ⎭ and AMOS BARTRAM, age 31, Cattle Drover, b. Staffs.	JOHN BURNE, age 21, born Roscommon, Ireland JOHN MOORE, age 20, born Roscommon, Ire. THOMAS DILLON, age 49, born Galloway. Ire. and WILLIAM H. BAYLIS, age 21, Wagoner, b. Worcs.

"Over here in England I'm helping with the hay,
An' I wisht I was in Ireland, the livelong day;
Weary on the English hay, an' 'sorra take the wheat—
Och! Corrymeela an' the blue sky over it!" *Moira O'Neill*

Haymakers pause for cider or beer dispensed by the boss. Only one glass is in evidence, to be passed round. For haymaking and harvest the men worked from dawn to dusk on piece-work, paid at so much an acre.

FUSTIAN was a favourite CLOTH for clothes of country people and manual workers.

Originally of Oriental origin, this strong and durable material, usually made of cotton in the Lancashire mills, had one side woven flat and the other cut to form a plush pile. The pile was cut after the cloth had been woven. A glue, which was later removed, held the pile in place while it was cut and it was then brushed to give a velvet-like appearance.

There were many different types of FUSTIAN:
e.g. moleskin, cantoon, velveteen, beaverteen, and

CORDUROY

which was first recorded in about 1795, origin of the name unknown, a ribbed fabric worn by practically all countrymen, and extremely hard-wearing. Trousers were worn every day for a year or more and never washed.

Corduroy was produced in many colours; fawn and brown were popular. Quarry workers favoured white, Lincolnshire "fenners" of the late 1880's liked bright blue. There were many patterns of ribbing.

Man in a fustian jacket and a neckerchief, photographed in Cambridgeshire about 1880

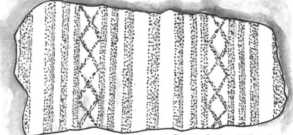

Regd. design 868048

A fancy fine white corduroy of about 1882

A countryman may be as warm in fustian as a king in velvet. *Old saying*

A boy of about 1885 in a complete corduroy suit, including corduroy leggings.

Horn-handled jack knives.

Men working in the fields ate their bread and cheese or salted pork by the "thumb-bit" method. They cut off a chunk which protruded beyond the thumb that held the "door-step" sandwich and they ate the chunk straight off the knife

A method of sharpening the knife was to hold the blade against the iron rim of a wagon wheel as it rotated.

1883 MONKTON FAIRLEIGH · Wiltshire. Farmer's son, S.G. Kendall, with his two brothers, was left in charge of the haymaking. His father had obtained, cheaply, some very strong old beer and they watered it down to give to the hay-makers, of which there were about 20 men and 4 or 5 women. Father went to Bristol and the sons doled out the diluted beer to the haymakers when they needed a drink.

Long before mid-day the brothers noticed that something was wrong with both the men and the women, who usually conducted themselves quietly. They were all cracking jokes, dancing about and making fools of themselves. Chaos reigned in the hay field and the brothers were compelled to call an end to the day's work. One brother was disgusted, another was almost hysterical with laughter at the drunken antics of the haymakers and the third blamed his father for not spending a bit more and buying some decent beer in the first place.

~Song of the Haymakers~   Eliza Cook

We dwell in the meadows, we toil on the sod,
  Far away from the city's dull gloom;
And more jolly are we, though in rags we may be
  Than the pale faces over the loom.
Then a song and a cheer for the bonny green stack,
  Climbing up to the sun wide and high;
For the pitchers, and rakers, and merry haymakers,
  And a beautiful Midsummer sky

A common practice at this time was to tie the neckerchief ends to the braces to prevent them from slipping off sideways

A farm SERVANT was hired on a yearly basis and often lived in.
A farm LABOURER lived away from the farm and was often married

One honest John Tomkins, a hedger and ditcher,
Although he was poor did not want to be richer;
For all such vain wishes to him were prevented
By a fortunate habit of being contented.

"For why should I grumble and murmer?" he said.
"If I cannot get meat I can surely get bread;
And though fretting may make my calamities deeper
It never can cause bread and cheese to be cheaper."

Jane Taylor (1783-1824)

Drawn from a photograph

A FEW TOOLS FAMILIAR TO THE FARM WORKER

DIBBER for making holes to sow seeds in (peas, beans, etc.)

DRAW HOE for loosening surface of soil and cutting away weeds

SLASHER for hedging and cutting tall growth

DUNG DRAG for pulling dung from a cart onto the land ready for spreading

STONE RAKE for clearing stones from a field

BILL HOOK for hedging

HOOK, slightly different shapes were made for different purposes: cutting corn, grass, brambles, furze, etc.

SACK HOOK for gripping and lifting full sacks

113

An enamelled metal badge

In 1906 the NATIONAL UNION of AGRICULTURAL WORKERS was formed. One of its aims was to give the farm worker a similar standard of living to the town worker.

Former Unions for agricultural workers had suffered from dwindling numbers, as hard times had made the workers too poor to pay the subscription. As they were scattered through the country and many lived in "tied" cottages, strikes for more wages could not be easily organised. In any case farmers could easily obtain help from non-union men who were only too pleased for an opportunity to earn a shilling or two.

The man having his hair cut wears leather straps below the knees of his trousers. They gave fullness to the trouser knees for easier bending and lifted the bottoms out of the mud. String or bands of straw were also used, or even, in East Anglia, eel skin, said to be more elastic, as well as protecting against rheumatism.

Village Barber

The straps were called by various names:
EIGHTSES ~ Suffolk, YORKERS ~ Dorset, KNEE-BELTS ~ Gloucestershire, JOSKINS ~ Yorkshire, also: LIGGETS, LALLYGAGS, EYE DUSTERS, ETC.

White shirts with a thin black stripe were popular in about 1910, often worn with a patent leather collar which could be wiped clean.

MANY LABOURERS WORE HATS THAT HAD BEEN PASSED ON TO THEM BUT BOOTS THEY USUALLY BOUGHT NEW

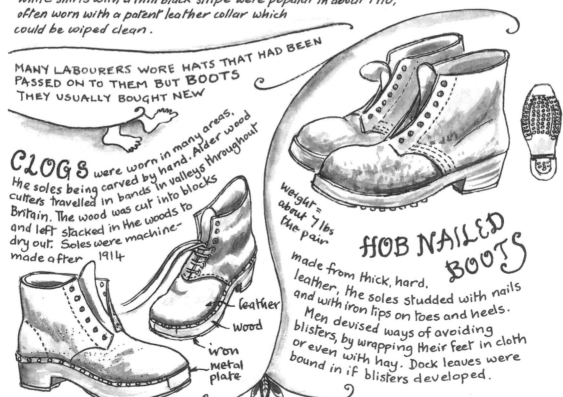

CLOGS were worn in many areas, the soles being carved by hand. Alder wood cutters travelled in bands in valleys throughout Britain. The wood was cut into blocks and left stacked in the woods to dry out. Soles were machine-made after 1914

leather
wood
iron metal plate

weight = about 7 lbs the pair

HOB NAILED BOOTS

made from thick, hard, leather, the soles studded with nails and with iron tips on toes and heels. Men devised ways of avoiding blisters, by wrapping their feet in cloth or even with hay. Dock leaves were bound in if blisters developed.

TOBACCO

provided one of few pleasures for the working man, He smoked it in a clay or briar pipe, or as a cigarette, which he often rolled himself, or he chewed it or took it as snuff.

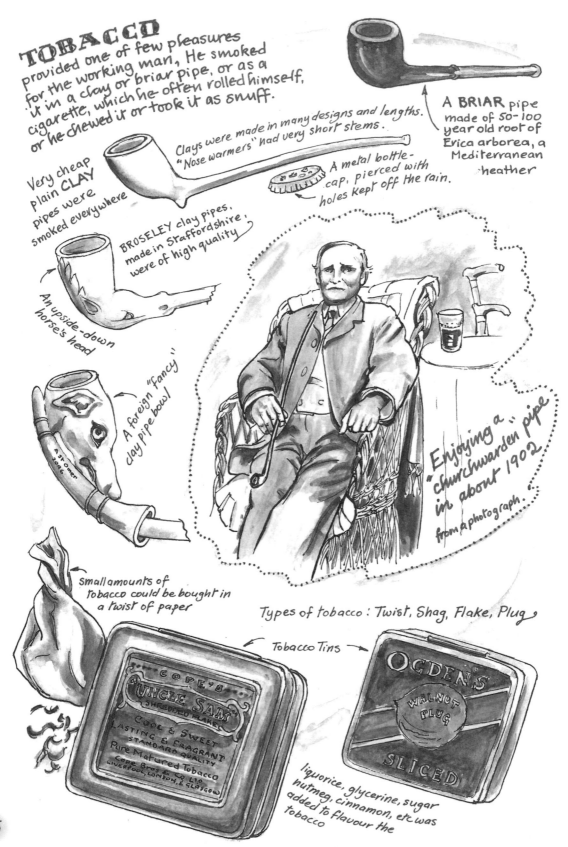

A BRIAR pipe made of 50-100 year old root of Erica arborea, a Mediterranean heather

Clays were made in many designs and lengths. "Nose warmers" had very short stems.

Very cheap plain CLAY pipes were smoked everywhere

A metal bottle-cap, pierced with holes kept off the rain.

BROSELEY clay pipes, made in Staffordshire, were of high quality

An upside-down horse's head

A foreign "fancy" clay pipe bowl

"Enjoying a "churchwarden" pipe in about 1902 from a photograph.

Small amounts of tobacco could be bought in a twist of paper

Types of tobacco: Twist, Shag, Flake, Plug,

Tobacco Tins

COPE'S "UNCLE SAM" SHREDDED FLAKES COOL & FRAGRANT LASTING & FRAGRANT STANDARD QUALITY Pure Matured Tobacco Cope Bros. & Co Ltd LIVERPOOL, LONDON & GLASGOW

OGDEN'S WALNUT PLUG SLICED

liquorice, glycerine, sugar, nutmeg, cinnamon, etc was added to flavour the tobacco

116

Men with a ginny ring, (gearing for grinding corn, etc), and the horse who walked in circles to turn it.

photograph taken on 7th July 1930, place unknown.

After the end of the War agricultural produce dropped in price, leaving farmers in financial difficulties. Many people were unemployed, whilst those fortunate enough to have work were paid low wages.

Before the War country people had been more or less content with their lives, but the war had widened their horizons. The agricultural labourers thought that they would like to have Saturday afternoons off, as well as Sundays, and a bicycle to ride to work on, while some even aspired to owning a motor-bike.

By the mid-1930's conditions for the labourers had improved. They were permitted seven days holiday with pay each year, but not more than three days could be taken at once.

Off-the-peg clothes became available everywhere. Distinctive locally made clothes disappeared

DUNGAREES (from Hindi: dungri, coarse calico), were worn in Britain from the early 1900s, soon overalls made from jean cloth became popular work-wear.

117

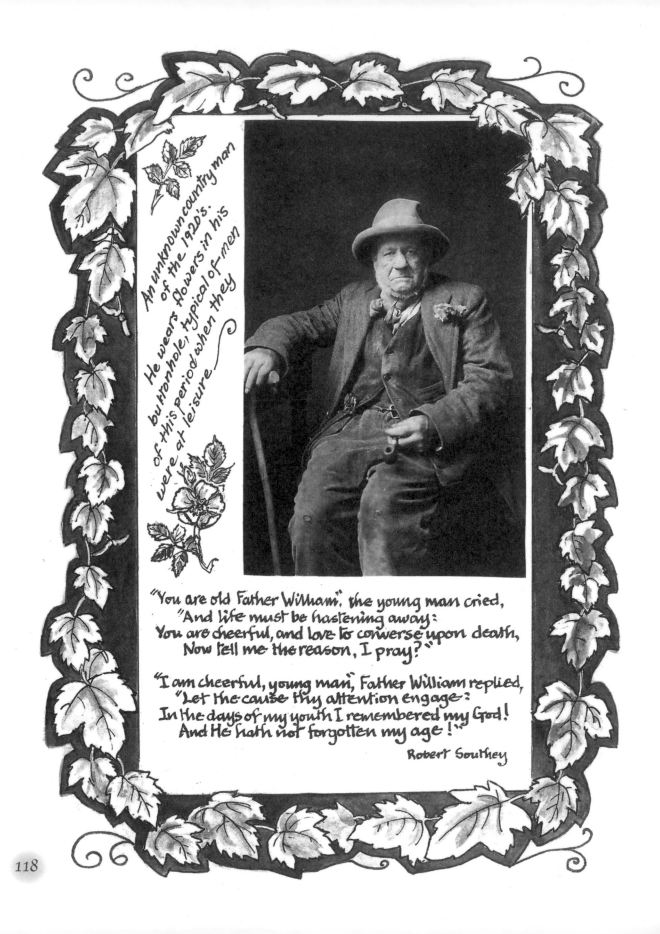

An unknown countryman of the 1920's. He wears flowers in his buttonhole, typical of men of this period when they were at leisure.

"You are old Father William", the young man cried,
  "And life must be hastening away:
You are cheerful, and love to converse upon death,
  Now tell me the reason, I pray?"

"I am cheerful, young man", Father William replied,
  "Let the cause thy attention engage:
In the days of my youth I remembered my God!
  And He hath not forgotten my age!"

Robert Southey

Child Labourers

" I used t'rise up wuth th' sun,
'Cos crows is arly bahds;
Full oft they've made me howl and run
An' say all kinds er words.
The more I scared, the more they teased,
An' kep' me on fer hours,
Till my poor feet, an' legs, an' knees
Had onmost lost their powers.

Car woo! car woo! yow owd black crow,
Goo fly awa' to Sutton;
If yow stop here t'll cost ye dear;
I'll kill ye dead as mutton."
                    Suffolk Song 1870's

From an early age children were
expected to earn a penny or two by
doing whatever work they could manage
in the fields.

Scaring the birds from the crops was one of the first tasks a
child was set to and he spent long and lonely days, from dawn to
dusk, seven days a week, acting as an animated scare crow in
the fields

LIPS, HOWEVER ROSY, MUST BE FED

At about ten years old a boy began regular work. Usually he was
hired by a nearby farmer, but some children stood at Hiring
Fairs with the adults, in the hope of someone offering employment

The BACK'US BOY (Back house) was low in the rural hierarchy.
He worked under the command of the farmer's wife and did any task
that she ordered. In a good house he could learn much before he
moved on to better paid work out of doors.

1846 Abingdon, Berkshire,

a sixteen year old boy who was working on a large farm earned three shillings a week.

"Three shillings!" exclaimed Alexander Somerville. "Have you nothing else? Don't you get victuals, or part of them from your master?"

"No. I buys them all."

"All out of three shillings?"

"Ees, and my clothes out of that."

"And what do you buy to eat?"

"Buy to eat! Why I buys bread and lard."

The boy had no place or time to boil vegetables but the master allowed him to boil potatoes once a week. He slept in a stable loft with five other hired hands. He was always too tired in the evenings to notice that his sheets were never washed and "I has to get up afore I be awake," so he didn't notice them in the mornings either.

OF A RAGGED COLT COMETH MANY A GOOD HORSE

about 1895

1903 West Riding, Yorkshire.

Fred Kitchen left school at thirteen and began as a "day-lad" on a 4-horse farm which was run by a widow. She also employed two "horse-chaps" and a cowman. Fred worked six days a week, twelve hours a day and he earned one shilling and three pence a day. He began as a crow scarer with three fields to cover. Then he stopped sheep from straying. He progressed to weeding corn, hoeing turnips and loading hay, where the men got him so drunk he was sent home. At harvest he twisted bands and tied sheaves and rode the leading horse drawing the binder. He picked apples and pears, helped with rick thatching and learned to plough, which he enjoyed.

The work of a farm boy remained much the same into the 1940's.

In the SECOND WORLD WAR young men were called up into the forces, leaving the land to be worked by those unfit for Service, older men, conscientious objectors, the Women's Land Army and anyone at all who had a few hours to spare. In the later war years Italian prisoners of war helped on the farms.

Digging for Victory, deep in the ground,
I thought of you, and look what I found!
for your — HAPPY BIRTHDAY!

In 1941 weekly wages for a male farm worker were about £2.8 shillings (£2·40)

Thousands of extra acres were ploughed to produce food, as imports were very limited.

On Christmas Day 1942 His Majesty King George VI addressed the country over the wireless. He said:

"We are thankful for the splendid addition to our food supplies made by those who work on the land and who have made it fertile and prolific as it has never been before."

By the end of the war mechanical equipment and tractors were increasingly used so the numbers of labourers and of horses declined rapidly.

Horses and a tractor ploughing together.

Women Workers

Women undertook a great many tasks on the land, particularly monotonous, repetitive work, such as stone-picking, hoeing, haymaking, fruit picking, harvest work, potato picking, etc.

Practical, plain and neat clothes, with a sun-bonnet, worn by a typical country woman in about 1900

Pea pickers in about 1897, when "leg-o-mutton" sleeves were at the height of fashion. These town women, wearing their town clothes, were brought out to the country by wagon or train, from nearby conurbations, returning home each evening

Women's work was seasonal and it varied according to the crops grown in the area. In districts where live-stock predominated there was no field work between hoeing in spring and hay making in late June/July.

Their hours were variable and very poorly paid. Men doing the same work were paid more

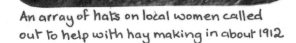

An array of hats on local women called out to help with hay making in about 1912

First World War 1914-18

When war broke out it was not realised at first by the government that a great deal of extra food would need to be grown, as imports would be difficult.

As a consequence 200,000 farm workers volunteered for the services early on and left the land. Later on another 200,000 were conscripted, leaving an inadequate work force.

The land was worked by the elderly, the unfit, service men on leave, prisoners of war and women.

A WOMENS LAND ARMY was formed in 1917, by which time food was desperately scarce. In 1918, at the end of the war, there were 23,000 in the WLA.

Cissie in March 1918 in Womens Land Army Uniform
from a photograph.

Polly, in uniform on a fine grey hunter.
photograph: M. Price Llangefni, Anglesey

Women met with many prejudices but their labour was valuable —

• JULY 1920 • "What an immeasurably wider view of things our Land Army days have given us. Out in the open air, with no one but ourselves and the sky, such a lot of room to think in, and nothing afraid to make us think, we have found thoughts in our hearts and minds that would never have dared show themselves in our old town days." Editor of The Landswoman.

Second World War 1939-45

In 1939 The WOMENS LAND ARMY was again formed, with the Hon. Director, Lady Denman of Balcombe Place, Sussex, giving over her home for the organisational headquarters.

Women from all walks of life found themselves engaged upon physically demanding farm work that had been considered previously as work for men. They spread dung, ploughed, drove tractors, caught rats, etc.

A special section of the WLA was the WOMENS TIMBER CORPS. The women felled and hauled trees and worked in saw mills.

Muriel wears her regulation hat (which the women rarely wore whilst working), and uniform of Aertex shirt, green jersey, brown breeches and fawn stockings. They were also issued with fawn overcoat, dungarees, gumboots, or boots and leggings.

JOAN MORRIS of Cannock, Staffordshire, did not enjoy working nights making nuts and bolts in a factory so Joan joined the Land Army and was sent to live in a hostel. From there she 'cycled out each day, often not knowing what work she would be assigned to.

The hostel, in Alcester, Warwickshire, accommodated about twenty women, four beds to a room, in two converted shops in the High Street. Joan earned 9 shillings a week, and a few of the women would pool their small change at the week-end to go to the pub. "We asked for three bottles of beer and eight glasses," she said.

Joan preferred market gardening and field work to dealing with animals. She worked in tomato houses around Salford Priors and Evesham. She picked sprouts in snow covered fields with fingers that were frozen and with chilblains on her feet. She worked all hours getting in the harvest and at threshing time.

"Oh! It was hard work but we had some good times," she declared.

A gang of Royal Marines, waiting to be demobbed, was sent to help out at the farm near Redditch where she was picking potatoes. They felt that they were being worked rather too hard and too long, so they sneaked some sugar into the tractor fuel tank in order to gain a respite.

Joan ended up marrying one of the Marines and she left the WLA at that time

from a postcard on which was written:
"I thought you would like to have this land girl, and to see her making the hay in knickers like a man. lots of kisses from Mummie."

Scarf tied as a turban

Regulation green jumper

Dungarees

Wellingtons for dirty work

TYPICAL WORKING CLOTHES

The Land Girls were billeted in hostels or they lived with their employer and his family, while some lodged near work with a landlady. Those who came from comfortable town homes were often shocked by primitive living conditions in the country, some found themselves on lonely farms with only a taciturn old labourer for every day company and a farmer who was doubtful about their abilities.

All the same, the majority who joined the WLA looked back afterwards on their farming days with pleasure. They were glad to have had the experience, although disappointed at the lack of recognition they received compared with the other Women's Services.

9 January 1945 · Farmer and Stockbreeder
Land Girl; able to take charge small dairy herd with assistance, model buildings, electric light, etc.
Duchess Farm, Clacton-on-Sea, Essex

24 April 1945 · Farmer and Stockbreeder
Land Girl; to take charge of two cows, manage the dairy and poultry; live in the house; work in garden in spare time. Reply with refs. to
Lady Katharine Meade, Hallgrove, Bagshot

125

HOP PICKERS

Hops are perennial and very sensitive plants, prone to disease. They improve the keeping quality of beer. The female plant bears the blossoms which have a sweet and heady scent and are ready for picking in late AUGUST/SEPTEMBER

mainly grown in KENT, SUSSEX, WORCESTERSHIRE, and some in Herefordshire, Hampshire, Surrey

In the photo the man on the left carries a sharp hook for cutting bines from the poles. In front of the women is a canvas "crib", "trough" or "bin" into which they stripped the flowers. In the foreground is a "poke" of hops ready to be taken to the kiln for drying

Photo. of about 1895, by Smith & Co., Clarendon Studio, Redhill, Surrey

126

ffop growers with small acreages usually hired local women to pick the crop. Sometimes gypsies were employed. Larger growers imported town families. In the south east Londoners went to the fields. In the Midlands the pickers came from the Black Country and Birmingham areas.

30 May 1857
Illustrated London News

HOP INTELLIGENCE.—The tenor of communications from the several hop-growing districts in Kent and Sussex is similar. The recent refreshing showers, though not sufficiently heavy to penetrate the parched ground deeply, have had a most beneficial effect on all the grounds. In Mid Kent the growth of the bine within the last few days is represented as being unparalleled, while the plants in most places are looking remarkably healthy, though still infested to some extent with the flea. In the Weald and in Sussex the change of weather has also produced a surprising effect, the bines in some of the young gardens having nearly topped the poles.

They were recruited by a local woman who arranged the transport by tram and wagon, and, later on, by lorry or coach

JS PF — Jeremiah Smith, Park Farm, Iden

RK — Richard Kenward. (for picking 12 bushels)

Metal tokens (Kent), paid to the pickers by the farmers. They could be exchanged for goods in shops and public houses.

WHOLE FAMILIES of GRANDMOTHERS, MOTHERS and CHILDREN went to pick for as long as six weeks at a time. They regarded it as a holiday for which they received payment. Living conditions were primitive. Barns, animal sheds and outhouses were swept out and freshly whitewashed in preparation for the women.

There were strict traditions and rules. The "tallyman", ("busheller" or "measureman") was master of ceremonies. He blew daily a horn to begin and to end picking and he measured in bushel amounts the quantities each had picked, often amidst ribaldry. Children picked into baskets, boxes, buckets, or upturned umbrellas and emptied them into their mothers' cribs

Londoners ready to go home at the end of picking. In the background can be seen the poles, now stripped of bines, in about 1900

Between 17,000 – 26,500 acres of hops were grown during the years 1920 – 1935

Hop picking by hand continued until about 1950 when machinery was brought in to harvest the crop. Town families usually retained fond memories of their summer "holidays" in the hop fields

127

WOODLAND WORKERS

Men took on forestry work particularly when they lived on, or near to, heavily wooded estates. They cleared land, planted, thinned out, transplanted and felled trees. The latter was dangerous work, needing judgement and experience.

← Cleaving thatch spars from hazel sticks. The spars are bent to hold down reed or straw thatch on buildings. Hazel is also used for hurdles, walking sticks, hedge stakes, etc.   photo H. Albino

In about 1900 this elderly man apparently donned his best clothes to have a photograph taken. He wears a tweed-fronted waist-coat and a voluminous sleeved shirt. The turned-up bottoms of his trousers reveal a lining

Stacked brushwood in the background indicates that he had been working in the coppices.

Axes only were used for tree-felling until about 1900, when saws came into use. The logs were pulled by horses to a hard road where they were hoisted onto a pole-wagon and hauled away to the saw pit.

Deciduous woods were planted for long-term felling

Conifer woods were planted to mature in less than 100 years.

A Timber Wagon

Trees were cut as close to the ground as possible. A wedge was first chopped out of the trunk on the side the tree was to fall, before starting to cut on the opposite side. Judgement of the wind was all important. The felling of a block of trees could create a wind tunnel, threatening to standing trees.

Cross-cutting with a saw required a team of two, all the work being done on the pull stroke

In 1919 the FORESTRY COMMISSION was established, with the aim of restoring native woodlands which had been denuded by the demand for wood during the First World War.

Wedges have been hammered into the saw-cut so that, when completely sawn through, the tree will fall away from them.

Wood had such a vast number of uses that, besides those men felling large timber, there were many others working on site in the woods, particularly in the winter months

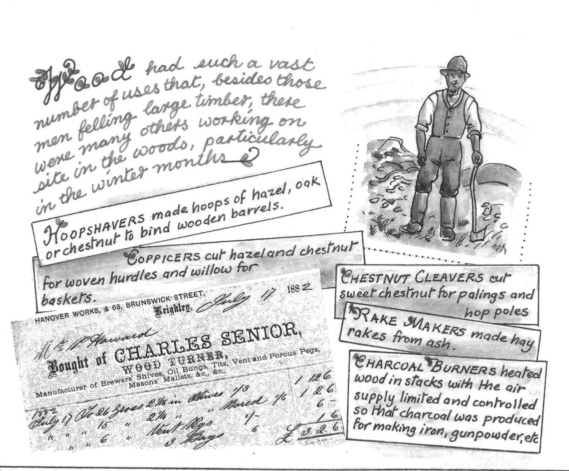

HOOPSHAVERS made hoops of hazel, oak or chestnut to bind wooden barrels.

COPPICERS cut hazel and chestnut for woven hurdles and willow for baskets.

CHESTNUT CLEAVERS cut sweet chestnut for palings and hop poles

RAKE MAKERS made hay rakes from ash.

CHARCOAL BURNERS heated wood in stacks with the air supply limited and controlled so that charcoal was produced for making iron, gunpowder, etc

HANOVER WORKS, & 68, BRUNSWICK STREET.
Keighley, July 17 1882

Mr P Howard
Bought of CHARLES SENIOR,
WOOD TURNER,
Manufacturer of Brewers' Shives, Oil Bungs, Tits, Vent and Porous Pegs, Masons' Mallets, &c., &c.

A Charcoal Burner's family outside a hut in which the charcoal burner lived. It was thatched with heather or turves. Extra accommodation in this case was provided by the caravan.

Foresters at Vaynol Park near Bangor

were paid the same rate as ordinary labourers.
In 1906 they received 2s 10d (14p) a day, plus extra
allowances, and overtime at 4d (1½p) an hour. The weekly
wage in England was between 13s 8d (68p) and 18s 0d (90p).

IN 1910 A LABOURER EARNED ABOUT THE SAME AS IN 1872

DOCTORS' CERTIFICATES for 3 of 37 Foresters employed on the Vaynol Estate, (owned by Charles Garden Assheton-Smith, Esquire).

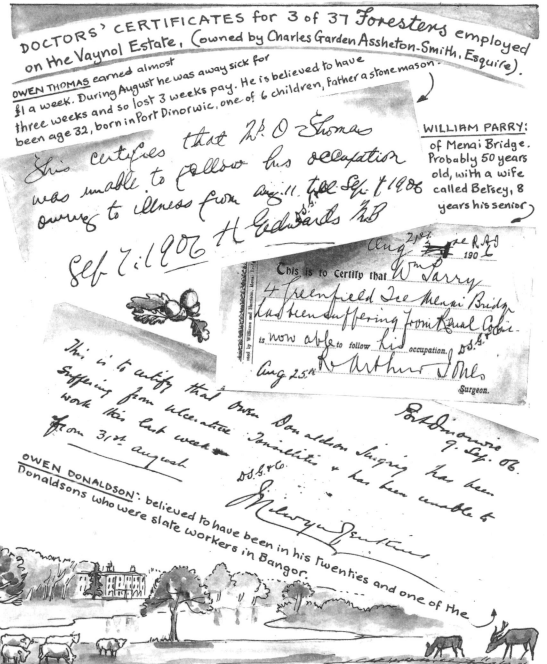

OWEN THOMAS earned almost
£1 a week. During August he was away sick for
three weeks and so lost 3 weeks pay. He is believed to have
been age 32, born in Port Dinorwic, one of 6 children, father a stone mason.

This certifies that Mr. O. Thomas
was unable to follow his occupation
owing to illness from Aug. 11 till Sep. 1 1906
Sep. 7th 1906 H. Edwards MB

WILLIAM PARRY:
of Menai Bridge.
Probably 50 years
old, with a wife
called Betsey, 8
years his senior.

Aug. 21st 1906
This is to Certify that Wm Parry
4 Greenfield Tce Menai Bridge
has been suffering from Renal Colic
is now able to follow his occupation.
Aug. 25th R. Arthur Jones
Surgeon.

This is to certify that Owen Donaldson Singing has been
suffering from Ulcerative Tonsilitis & has been unable to
work this last week
from 31st August
D.S.G.&Co.

Port Dinorwic
9. Sep. 06.

OWEN DONALDSON: believed to have been in his twenties and one of the
Donaldsons who were slate workers in Bangor.

VILLAGERS

There's a butcher's, and a carpenter's, and a plumber's
    and a small greengrocer's and a baker,
But he won't bake on a Sunday, and there's a sexton
    that's a coal merchant besides, and an undertaker.
And a toyshop, but not a whole one, for a village can't
    compare with London shops;
One window sells drums, dolls, kites, carts, bats,
    clout's balls, and the other sells malt and hops.
And Mrs. Brown, in domestic economy not to be a
    bit behind her betters,
Lets her house to a milliner, a watchmaker, a
    ratcatcher, a cobbler, lives in it herself, and it's
        the post office for letters.
Now I've gone through all the village— aye, from the
    end to end, save and except for one more house,
But I haven't come to that— and I hope I never
    shall — and that's the Village Poor House.

A VERSE FROM "OUR VILLAGE". T. HOOD

A carrier outside The White Horse, (proprietor Frederick Askew), in Shere, Surrey, about 1905

The CARRIER carried almost anything that was not too large, including people. He would collect butter and eggs from farms and deliver them to shops in towns and he took goods to and from railway stations, etc. He was the link between towns and villages and he relayed news between them, too.

132

A TRAVELLING SHOW of what appears to be PUPPETS on a platform, travelling the road from Deal to Dover, 1904

A group of MUSICIANS. (unknown location)

Entertainment

MAY DAY at school, 1920's, with singing, flowers and a maypole.

A gardener with a curly-coated retriever type of dog in the late 1800's

In about 1870, Bridport, Dorset, this man looks fondly at his little pet, who wears a brass collar.

{ MEN and DOGS }

After the end of the war, in the late 1940's, these men have spent an enjoyable hour or two catching rats with the aid of the dog. Two of the men are wearing old uniform jackets.

About 1900. These two seem to be well matched, with a resemblance to one another.

If a woman left her house for a short while she often left the key outside in the lock. This indicated that she did not intend to be away for very long.

Brackenhurst Cottage near Astwood Bank, Worcestershire. (demolished 1960's)

A TYPICAL COUPLE of the 1890's
She wears a ribbon-trimmed bonnet, plaid shawl and a pretty tucked apron.

He wears fustian trousers and a heavy overcoat buttoned up to the neck.

I've dwelt in my cot for many long years,
And rubb'd through life mid smiles and tears;
It's as queer an old pile as you ever did see,
But does very well for my old man and me.
There's a purling spring in the lane below,
Which vary's not in it's ebb and flow;
Our boys ran there, and drank so free,
And there it remains for the old man and me.
Our struggles and pleasures will soon be o'er,
And we shall need the cot no more;
Ah! others around the hearthstone will be,
In this cot long so dear to the old man and me.

George Evans 1875

A Cottager and his Wife

about 1895

He wears a sleeved waist-coat, a garment popular with country workers. His hands are broad and gnarled, indicating a life of outdoor work

She wears a plain dress with decorative gathered cuffs, and a crocheted woollen shawl, an ubiquitous garment at that time. Her cap is of pleated ribbon and she favours a velvet ribbon across her forehead

The country village in the late 1800's housed people with occupations that made the village almost self sufficient, for example:

parson, school master, inn keeper, butcher, tailor, baker, grocer, general dealer, gardener, shoe maker, blacksmith, wheelwright, harness maker, miller, hurdlemaker, draper, police officer, postmaster, dressmaker, laundress, field worker, charwoman and perhaps a cattle dealer, fish hawker, builder, etc.

Village Miscellany

A family with a Bagot goat, photographed in Leigh, Lancashire in about 1885.

OLD AGE PENSIONS were introduced on 1st January 1909 by David Lloyd George, the Chancellor of the Exchequer, for those aged over 70. This removed their fear of having to enter the workhouse.

Flat-topped head gear; protective shoulder sacking, bandaged right hand; he may have worked with stone.

A young policeman called Walter in 1912.

OUTDOOR BONNETS

Bonnets were worn by country women throughout the 19th century. Both men and women wore head-coverings outdoors. To go out without a hat was considered to be "not the done thing," especially for adults. Although bonnets went out of fashion by 1900, hats were almost always worn until about 1945.

A "best" bonnet in dark material, in a similar pattern to those worn in the fields. From a carte-de-visite by Wm. Ferguson, Keswick taken in the 1870's

a smart bonnet of the 1840's

Bonnets came in many styles. Most had frills and ruching and a "curtain" to protect the back of the neck

with a little brim of soft cotton, c.1885

a soft brim, worn turned back, c.1890

ruching and frills, beautifully stitched about 1890 (Museum of English Rural Life).

138

Traditional bonnet and shawl

A housemaid has her fortune told by a gypsy calling at the back door.

Until the First World War, the *Village Girl* usually went into service with a family that could afford to have help. Sometimes she would be the only employee, carrying out all manner of lowly household tasks. Sometimes her mother might pay a few pennies a week for her training in a good class household for a year, after which she received a wage. Her expectation in life was to marry and to have a family.

The Womens' Institute

THE WOMENS' INSTITUTE was founded in Canada in 1897 as an offshoot of The Farmers' Institute. Despite attempts to interest Britain in the idea, it was not until the 1914-18 War broke out that the first WI was started in Britain, in June 1915 in Llanfairpwll, North Wales. The chairman of the North Wales Agricultural Organisation lived in that area.

The WI was formed to encourage the participation of countrywomen in the production and preservation of foodstuffs. The Institutes spread to villages Nationwide and, after the War, continued. The WI brought countrywomen together for regular meetings centred upon rural concerns.

The INN KEEPER

George Fame and his wife, licenced to sell beer by retail in about 1870

(Painted lozenge, old customary sign of a tavern).

Beersellers, Keepers of Taverns and Inns were a part of village and town life from time immemorial, with the public house as much a part of village life as the church.

According to the size of the establishment the landlord's business was to make his guests happy with everything, from a friendly word and ale to a hearty dinner, and a bed and stabling for the horse. A woman, often a widow, might run a public house herself, with family or hired help, or a married woman might be hostess whilst her husband followed another occupation.

PUBLIC HOUSE NAMES recall many historical and traditional events

The WHITE HORSE
Standard of the Saxons

The BARLEY MOW
Harvest and making Malt for beer

The ANCHOR
Keep Safe
Symbol of Christian Faith

The GREEN MAN
May Day figure, Rebirth

The PLOUGH
Plough Monday - First Mon. 12 days after Christmas

"Where'ere his fancy bids him roam,
In every inn he finds a home,
Should fortune change her fav'ring wind,
Though former friends should prove unkind,
Will not an inn his cares beguile
Where on each face he sees a smile?"
William Combe.

A carefully posed photograph, about 1905, showing the delights of the public house: beer, smoking, dominos, cards and good company

140

The Miller took in grain from local farmers and returned the flour to them. If the mill was wind-driven it was idle on calm days. A water-mill was more reliable as long as the watercourses remained open and they did not dry up in a severe drought.

The Miller

He had to keep a continual check to see that the grain ran neither too fast nor too slowly to the millstones, and that the grooves in the stones did not clog with flour

A Miller's Wagon at Heckfield, Hampshire. (Lithograph by C. White)

Mill stones that ran without corn between them grew hot and could cause a fire

Millstone

By 1900 most wind and water mills had ceased operating and grain was processed by steam and mechanised mills.

THE PARSON

And he was kind, and loved to sit
  In the low hut or garnished cottage
And praise the farmer's homely wit,
  And share the widow's homelier pottage:
At his approach complaint grew mild;
  And when his hand unbarred the shutter,
The clammy lips of fever smiled
  The welcome which they could not utter.

                     W. Mackworth Praed.

The Parson and the Squire were often the only two men in the district who were well educated until a school-master became part of the village community. Clergymen were drawn from the upper class families and had been brought up to follow country pursuits and to play games such as cricket and croquet.

A parson with a rural background could sympathise with parishioners from all backgrounds and they were involved in most things that happened in the village. Many were social reformers who tried to obtain better conditions for the poor local people.

Some parsons were eccentric, some took to drink, many enjoyed shooting, fishing and hunting. With few other people to talk to in the vicinity who were of a similar educational standard, many kept diaries, or studied and became authorities on a variety of subjects, for example:

• Robert Stephen Hawker, 1803-1875, Morwenstowe, Cornwall, fought for higher wages for labourers, wrote poetry, including the song "And Shall Trelawney Die," and, in 1843, introduced the Harvest Festival.

• John Mossop, 1830-1873, Covenham, Lincolnshire, was a pioneer of British Ornithology.

• Octavius Pickard-Cambridge, 1848-1917, a Squarson of Bloxworth, Dorset, published two volumes on "The Spiders of Dorset"

• Sabine Baring Gould, 1834-1924, Lewtrenchard, Devon, was a best-selling novelist and wrote many non-fiction works, including "Old Country Life" and a collection of English Folk Songs, also the hymn "Onward Christian Soldiers".

• Charles Kingsley, 1819-1875, Eversley, Hampshire, was famous for his socialist novels, which included "The Water Babies" and "Westward Ho."

• Francis Kilvert 1840-1879, Clyro, Radnorshire, kept a diary rich in the description of people and places in his area.

The Sexton

The work of the Sexton was the care of the church and its church-yard, in which he dug the graves when the villagers died.

"I delve, I delve in the earth full deep
A bed for the troubled mourner's sleep;
And dark and lonesome, dank and dread,
The clay-cold couch I smooth for the dead;
Yet, though noisome, dank and dreat
No voice of complaint from the dead's heat;
Each is content in his narrow room
The graveyard gives calm till the Day of Doom.

Knight Hunt

a SEXTON
dressed in his Sunday best

Bought flowers were first seen at funerals
in about 1870

The dead are buried with the feet to the east so that when they rise up on the Day of Judgement they face the Lord. A parson is buried with feet to the west so that when he rises up he will be facing his flock.

143

Village Children

Wooden-soled clogs were popular in northern England as well as in many other areas.

1884

Annie Wena of Pwllheli, North Wales in 1910

This Welsh girl knits a stocking on four needles. She wears the traditional costume of hat with a shawl and apron. The hat was popular wear for Welsh women in the 1850's when it was both taller and narrower. In the 1830's leaders of the Welsh Revival had deliberately designated the hat and cloak as the National Costume for Welsh women.

When they were not working or were at school or Sunday school village children had the country-side for their playground. Most of their waking hours were spent outside. According to the season, they made and tried out catapults, fished, went birds' nesting, went "scrumping" fruit, paddled in streams, slid on frozen ponds, explored woods, tormented animals, hung onto the backs of carts and generally made a nuisance of themselves as they made their own amusement with whatever came to hand.

• SCHOOL •

In 1880 it became compulsory for all children between the ages of 5 and 10 to attend school.

1893 · The minimum leaving age was 11, which was raised to 12 in 1899

A Schoolroom in Caterham, Surrey, about 1910

With Grandfather

Isle of Wight
about 1915

about 1925

145

GYPSIES

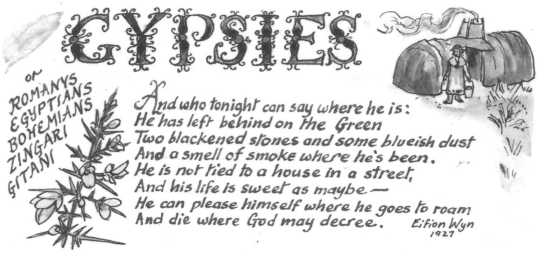

or
ROMANYS
EGYPTIANS
BOHEMIANS
ZINGARI
GITANI

And who tonight can say where he is:
He has left behind on the Green
Two blackened stones and some blueish dust
And a smell of smoke where he's been.
He is not tied to a house in a street,
And his life is sweet as maybe —
He can please himself where he goes to roam
And die where God may decree.   Eifion Wyn
                                          1927

The GYPSIES arrived in England in about 1500, having originated in Northern India. They spoke the Romany language, based on Sanskrit and they gradually assimilated English and Welsh words.

Ordinary people were suspicious and fearful of them. They were outlandish and rough, living in tents as they travelled. They made no plans or provisions from one day to the next and had no desire to stay in one place or to live in houses. They preferred the open air.

They travelled on foot, sometimes with a donkey to carry the poles and blankets which they set up as BENDER TENTS. When road surfaces improved some afforded a cart to carry belongings. The cart itself provided a place underneath for sleeping.

They usually travelled in regular circuits of the country. Some family groups might travel the South East, others might keep to Yorkshire, some to the New Forest, etc.

They left messages (pattran) on the road for other gypsies to find. They were in the form of arrangements of twigs and straw, tufts of grass, pebbles, or perhaps a fragment of cloth tied to a tree to indicate a direction

Gypsy Woman with a Baby   1860   by W. Keyl

146

SOME WOMENS' NAMES ~
STARLINA, DAMARIS, NATION, DARKLIS, RICHENDA, ROSA, CORALINA, ESTHER, ALABINA, EVERGREEN, MERENDA, URSULA, MORELLA, VASHTI, SYNFYE, LYDIA

BOSWELL, INGRAM, WOOD, LEE, BUCKLAND, HERON, SMITH, LOVELL, STANLEY, JONES, LOVERIDGE
~ SOME SURNAMES ~

A Wagon Lamp

"You've got a lucky face lady"

SARAH BOSWELL, age 99, with her grand daughter, photographed near Blackpool in about 1900

chrysanthemum
shaved elder
privet stalk
tin from a tin can
split willow
CHRYSANTHEMUM PEGS

Many marriages were arranged by the parents and they married within their own tribe. They kept apart from ordinary people ("gorgios"). They held traditional ceremonies but were often married and buried at church.
The Romany man was in charge. The woman obeyed him. He beat her if she did not. Only when past child-bearing age was she respected

The women went hawking round villages and farms with baskets of spring flowers, heather, herbs, clothes pegs, and wooden chrysanthemum flowers. They sold anything that they could find or make: baskets, beeskeps of straw bound with bramble and so on. They begged for old clothes, food, or anything at all that might come in useful, and they told fortunes.

As o'er my palm the silver piece she drew,
And traced the line of life with piercing view,
How throbb'd my fluttering pulse with hopes and fears,
To learn the colour of my future years. SAMUEL ROGERS. 1792

HOAR FROST AND GYPSIES NEVER STAY NINE DAYS IN ONE PLACE

When a place was found to stop, the children collected sticks for the fire. The men removed turf for the fireplace and set up the kettle prop; the women tied the food into separate bags, ready to boil together in the cooking pot. They hoped the police would not appear and move them on.

Gypsies from all over the country gathered at annual FAIRS for meeting friends, fighting enemies and horse-trading at BROUGH, APPLEBY, YARM, BRIG, STOW-ON-THE-WOLD, BARNET and EPSOM for Derby Week.

It was not until after the 1850's that the gypsies began living in wagons, and it was about 1870 before these were fitted with a bed, cupboards, seats and a stove. The special, craftsman-built and highly decorated wagons appeared in the late 1800's

WAGON (VARDO)

BOW TOP

READING

LEDGE

OPEN LOT
(after 1930)

CLOTHES were mostly cast-offs begged from respectable households and so they were in the current fashions of the time. The gypsy women wore them in their own unconventional way by combining garments and colours that ordinary people would not wear together.

They loved bright scarves and they added feathers, frills, fringes and jewellery

A man would buy new clothes for "best" if he could afford them

black velour hat (no dent)

"diklo", bright silk neckerchief

Jacket, often brown or green, with decorative stitching on pockets and lapels, and with an internal breast pocket and a poacher's pocket.

moleskin or corduroy trousers

GYPSY GENTLEMAN (ROMANY RAI) about 1900

GYPSY STYLE

1915

1910

1920's

1930

For Best Holiday Attire a wealthy gypsy man in the late 1800's might wear a bright plush waistcoat with sleeves and with buttons of silver or made from golden guineas. An everyday waistcoat was often of leather. A cloak made of skins riveted together gave a wild and rich effect. He wore earrings, rings and sometimes bracelets. A large pocket watch might be displayed, even if he did not know how to tell the time.

Coral, jade, and amber were special favourites for beads and brooches, and gold sovereigns were made into rings.

Women favoured elaborate plaited arrangements for their hair in the early 1900's. They treated it with mutton fat or butter to make it shining and sleek

149

The gypsies' FOOD consisted of anything that they could find, catch or steal, together with some bought items, such as flour, sugar and tea. They ate birds, animals and fish that were large enough to be worth preparing, even carrion (moulo maso), hedge-hogs (hotchi-witchi) and snails (bourri) roasted or as soup (zimmins). Vegetables they stole from fields.

They kept LURCHER DOGS, quiet, obedient and very fast, to catch hares and rabbits. The lurcher was specially bred, from a greyhound or other running dog which was crossed with a working dog, such as a collie, to give both speed and intelligence.

Dog (jukal)

Any animal that licked its own fur was considered "unclean". This included dogs, animals very necessary to the gypsy's life. Hands had to be washed after handling a dog.

Horses were "clean". Utensils licked by them could be used by a human being

Gypsies especially liked piebald and skewbald horses

HORSES were their WEALTH

Horse (grei)

"GYPSY GOLD DOESN'T CHINK AND GLITTER, IT GLEAMS IN THE SUNLIGHT AND NEIGHS IN THE DARK"

GOOD LUCK (cushgar bok)

Gypsies survived by their wits, by horse-dealing, poaching, petty thieving, always being ready to do a deal in anything. They took seasonal work on farms, especially fruit and hop picking.

150

Tinkers

Tinkers, or Tinklers were itinerants who had usually originated in Ireland or Scotland. They lived and travelled in a similar way to Gypsies but their origins and traditions were completely different.

In the early 1850's, when travelling in Wales, George Borrow asked:
"What kind of people are these "Gwyddelod?" (Irish Tinkers)
"Savage, brutish people, sir, in general without shoes and stockings, with coarse features and heads of hair like mops."
"How do they live?"
"The men tinker a little, sir, but more frequently plunder. The women tell fortunes and steal whenever they can!"
"They live something like the Gipsiaid?"
"Something, sir, but the hen Gipsiaid were gentle folks by comparison."

♪♫ Their music was Celtic-based folk music. They had their own language of Shelta, sometimes called "Bog Latin" or "The Ould Thing". Some could also speak Gammon, a thieves' slang or cant.

repaired with a patch of tin.

The Irish Tinkers were Roman Catholics. They made and repaired pots and pans and any tin-ware articles, they dealt in horses, did road mending, took seasonal farm work, sharpened knives and scissors, etc. Like the gypsies, they slept in tents or barrel-topped wagons. They liked to drink 'Guinness' and 'poteen', an Irish whiskey which they brewed themselves.

Hawkers or Pedlars

Hawkers travelled for miles on foot, carrying heavy packs out into the countryside from the towns where they had stocked up on wares that would please country people.

The farmers' wives, who rarely went to shops in town, generally welcomed them. Usually they parted with a few pennies for combs, needles, thread, ribbons, lace, a piece of cheap jewellery or other pretty trinket. The Pedlars' Act of 1871 required that they be licensed by the police.

151

TRAMPS

"I know not where the white road leads, nor what the blue hills are,
But a man can have the sun for a friend, and for his guide a star,
And there's no end of voyaging when once the voice is heard,
For the river calls and the road calls, and oh! the call of a bird!"

Gerald Gould. 1885-1936

TRAMPS, or VAGABONDS, walked the roads from April to November. There were a few women tramping, but usually they were penniless men, perhaps old soldiers, or without family, or simply people unable to settle down.

They walked the roads in an aimless way, but some appeared from time to time in districts they had visited before, even staying for months in a cave or derelict building where they had been before.

Many enjoyed the life and most walked alone, only occasionally teaming up with another for a short period. They were independent characters who liked a solitary life and preferred to be out in the open air. If invited into a house to eat they preferred to stay out of doors.

They slept outside in dry weather or, on wet nights, in the lee of a haystack or in farm buildings. In winter time they usually disappeared from the countryside and went into doss houses or hostels in towns, or into a workhouse. If they had relations they might stay with them. A few stayed out all winter and were occasionally found dead from exposure to cold.

When 'on the road' they sometimes encountered one another at certain places that were good overnight stopping spots, or in public houses, known to them as "boose cribs".

They carried a few personal possessions wrapped in a bundle: a billy can in which to brew tea, a tin mug, a clay pipe, (in which they might smoke old tea leaves), and a plug of tobacco to chew.

In the 1920's-30's the numbers of tramps were swelled by men who had become unemployed during the Depression, but they were hoping to find work and so were not tramps by choice

Tramps lived by various means whilst they travelled. The higher the original position of the man in society, the lower he was likely to sink, for he was hesitant about begging or entering a workhouse. Others had their own methods of making a few pennies:

The DOWN-RIGHTER ~ was a straight-forward beggar, asking for money, etc. A tramp might do well at a popular picnic spot. A tramp in East Anglia said that if he waited "near to where they were a-goffin" and then walked past, feigning a limp whilst bidding the people an affable 'good-day', he was likely to be given a sandwich or a piece of cake. *S.L.Bensusan*

The GRIDLER ~ sang hymns in the town square in a shaking voice. Sometimes he borrowed a poor-looking child, making people give because they felt sorry for him. According to W.H.Davies, the Gridler was at the top of the profession because he had a skill of sorts and he did not have to carry any stock with him.

The HAWKER ~ carried a few bootlaces or berries and flowers that he had collected. He offered them for sale but hoped people would give him money and not take them away from him, or he would have to go and collect more.

The KNIFE-GRINDER pushed a sharpening stone on wheels 'round the country, travelling to villages, remote farms and cottages. He called: "Knives and Scissors to Grind, O," and people brought them out for sharpening.

The MOOCHER or MOUCHER ~ picked up anything he could from field and hedgerow which he could sell. He collected such things as black-berries, water-cress, nuts or mushrooms. Moss and sprays of box and ivy he could sell to florists' shops.
Writing in *The Gentleman's Magazine*, July 1890, 'Peregrinus' tells of "Mickey the Moucher" who was looked upon as one of the best "cadgers" on the road. Like all of his class, he resented any poaching on his preserves - that is at his "good cribs." He had a reputation of knowing every house that was "good for a couldprafie" in the counties of Oxford, Berkshire, Wiltshire, Somerset, and Gloucestershire.

The SEASONAL LABOURER ~ took farm jobs for short periods when the fancy took him, but he soon tramped onwards when he had earned enough to buy tobacco and beer.

NUMBERS DWINDLED after 1945. With the introduction of the WELFARE STATE ordinary people were not as generous and ready to give as they had been formerly. The tramps could now obtain Relief.

BIBLIOGRAPHY

Tallyman (Hop Picking)

BILLET Michael. A History of English Country Sports, Robert Hale 1994
BONSER J.S.   The Drovers   MacMillan & Co. Ltd   1970
BORROW George   Lavengro.   Romany Rye, John Murray 1900
BOSWELL S.G. ed. John Seymour. The Book of Boswell, Gollancz 1970
BRANDER Michael. A Concise Guide to Game Shooting, Sportsman's Press 1986
BRILL Edith, Life & Tradition in the Cotswolds, J.M. Dent   1973
CARLEY Gaius. The Memoires of a Sussex Blacksmith   1963
CAUNCE Stephen. Amongst Farm Horses Alan Sutton   1991
CHIVERS Keith.   The Shire Horse   Futura   1978
DAVIES Jennifer. Tales of the Old Horsemen, David & Charles   1997
DAVIES W.H. Autobiography of a Supertramp, Jonathan Cape 1950
ERNLE Lord. English Farming Past and Present, Longmans Green 1936
EVANS George Ewart. The Horse in the Furrow Faber and Faber 1960
EVANS George Ewart. Where Beards Wag All   Faber & Faber   1970
GWYER Joseph Gwyers Life and Poems, 4th Ed. author   1877
GROVES Reg.   Sharpen the Sickle   Porcupine Press   1948
HARVEY Denis.   The Gypsies   B.T. Batsford   1979
HEATH Francis George. Peasant Life in the West of England. Sampson Law 1880
HORN Pamela.   The Victorian Country Child Sutton Publishing   1974
HUDSON W.H.   A Shepherd's Life   Methuen & Co
JACKSON Alastair.   The Great Hunts   David & Charles   1989
KEEGAN Terry.   The Heavy Horse   Pelham Books   1973
KENDAL S.G. Farming Memoirs of a West Country Yeoman. Faber & Faber 1944
KITCHEN Fred.   Brother to the Ox   Caliban Books   1981
LANSDELL Avril. Fashion à la Carte 1860-1890 Shire Publications   1985
LEWIS June. The Cotswolds, Life & Traditions   Weidenfeld & Nicolson   1996
MOBBS A.G. (preface) Facts & Incidents of an Unequal Struggle.
                    Ashford, Kent and Sussex Tithepayers Association c 1950
MURSELL Norman. Fifty Years a Gamekeeper   Allen & Unwin   1981
NICHOLSON Marie G. Portrait of a Victorian Gentleman: James Ruffin Blake. m/s 1978
PORTER Valerie.   Yesterday's Countryside   David & Charles   2000
RAWLINGS. Leslie. Gamekeeper: Memories of a Country Childhood. Boydell Press 1997
RIDLEY Jane.   Fox Hunting   Collins   1990
SACKVILLE-WEST V.   The Women's Land Army   Michael Joseph   1944
SAMPSON J (editor).   Wind on the Heath   Chatto & Windus   1930
SOMERVILLE Alexander. The Whistler at the Plough. Ainsworth 1852 rep.1989
TOULSON Shirley.   The Drovers   Shire Publications No. 45
VESEY FITZGERALD Brian. Gypsies of Britain David & Charles   1973
VINCE John.   Shepherding   Sorbus   1990's
WALSH E.G. (editor). The Poacher's Companion   The Boydell Press   1983
WEBBER Ronald.   The Village Blacksmith   David & Charles   1971
WILLS Barclay. Shepherds of Sussex   Skeffington & Son Ltd   c. 1935
YOUATT William.   The Dog   Longmans Green & Co   1895